TAKING YOUR READERS

ON A HERO'S JOURNEY

BRYAN DAVIS

BOOKS BY BRYAN DAVIS

The Reapers Trilogy
Reapers
Beyond the Gateway
Reaper Reborn

Let the Ghosts Speak

Time Echoes Trilogy
Time Echoes
Interfinity
Fatal Convergence

Dragons in our Midst
Raising Dragons
The Candlestone
Circles of Seven
Tears of a Dragon

Oracles of Fire
Eye of the Oracle
Enoch's Ghost
Last of the Nephilim
The Bones of Makaidos

Children of the Bard
Song of the Ovulum
From the Mouth of Elijah
The Seventh Door
Omega Dragon

Dragons of Starlight
Starlighter
Warrior
Diviner
Liberator

Tales of Starlight
Masters & Slayers
Third Starlighter
Exodus Rising

Wanted: Superheroes
Wanted: A Superhero to Save the World
Hertz to Be a Hero
Antigravity Heroes

To learn more about Bryan's books, go to
www.daviscrossing.com

Facebook - facebook.com/BryanDavis.Fans

Write Them In: Taking Your Readers on a Hero's Journey

Copyright © 2020 by Bryan Davis

Published by Scrub Jay Journeys
P. O. Box 512
Middleton, TN 38052
www.scrubjayjourneys.com
email: info@scrubjayjourneys.com

All rights reserved. No part of this publication may be reproduced, distributed, or transmitted in any form or by any means, including photocopying, recording, or other electronic or mechanical methods, without the prior written permission of the publisher, except in the case of brief quotations embodied in critical reviews and certain other noncommercial uses permitted by copyright law.

ISBN Print: 978-1-946253-03-3
ISBN Epub: 978-1-946253-04-0
ISBN Mobi: 978-1-946253-05-7

First Printing – February 2020

Printed in the U.S.A.
Library of Congress Control Number: 2020900004

Introduction

Readers want to be part of an adventure, to travel on a journey of mind and emotion. They long to raise a gleaming sword with Samwise Gamgee against Shelob the spider, to ride with Lucy on Aslan's back and feel his silky mane, or to wield a light saber in fierce combat on a planet in a galaxy far, far away.

As writers, we hope to fulfill that literary longing, to immerse readers in a story they won't want to leave. Once they do resurface in their real worlds, they will be eager to return to ours, whether through the same story or others we have written. And they will be sure to tell friends about their journeys and invite new readers to enter our fascinating worlds.

To create this emotional bonding between a reader's mind and a story's journey, we need to accomplish three basic steps:

1. Tell a story that includes a captivating journey.
2. Create characters with whom readers can emotionally connect.
3. Employ writing techniques that draw readers into a scene and keep them there.

To help you accomplish these goals, I will describe the basic elements of the hero's journey story structure. During the description of an element, I will introduce ways authors can establish emotional connections between characters and readers. Finally, after I complete the journey's elements, I will provide a toolbox of techniques that will help you write readers into the scenes.

When you complete all three steps, your readers will feel like they're on the journey, one that we hope they will never forget.

Let's start with a short description of the journey's story structure.

The Hero's Journey

There are many story genres: romance, horror, mystery, fantasy, science-fiction, and so on. Although these can vary greatly in content, a particular structure often appears regardless of the genre—The Hero's Journey.

Many have written about The Hero's Journey, describing its building blocks in a number of ways with terminology that differs from writer to writer. Some mention the hero's early refusal to go on the journey. Others discuss the hero's return to the ordinary world with a healing elixir. And we often hear about the hero's death and rebirth either in a physical or spiritual sense, perhaps both.

While these elements can be intriguing parts of a hero's journey, they are not all necessary elements. In order to provide a structure that will be suitable for almost any genre, I will describe a basic version of The Hero's Journey that includes only the structure's essentials. I will also use terms that differ from other descriptions you might have seen.

For the sake of brevity and simplicity, I will use the term *hero* for a male or female heroic character, and I will usually choose male pronouns.

See page 6 for a diagram of the basic structure. The story starts in the lower left corner, in the hero's ordinary world. Follow the arrows to proceed through the structure to the end of the map.

I call the diagram a map, because it provides a writing path that will help you both start and finish your story. Many aspiring authors have great ideas, but they might not know where to start or, once they have started, what to do next or how to finish. This map provides reminders to guide them toward completion.

For example, once you have written a crisis event that drastically alters the ordinary world, you need to establish a goal that will send your hero on a pursuit of that goal. Then a conflict with the villain should arise to temporarily halt the journey. After that, the hero must continue the pursuit, armed with the wisdom and experience that the conflict bestowed.

And so the map continues, step by step by step.

If that's confusing, don't worry. Every step will be described in detail as this book proceeds.

While you read, it might help to return to the diagram from time to time to remind yourself of your location on the map. That way, the elements of the journey will be implanted in your mind, and writing this kind of story will become more natural as you practice it.

Are you ready for the journey? Let's get started.

The Ordinary World

We start the story in the hero's ordinary world—his normal way of life, his geographical home, his occupation, etc. As readers watch the hero in this setting, they will get to know him and, we hope, create an emotional attachment to him.

Since the first step in the journey is crucial with regard to getting your readers engaged, we will spend more time on it than any other.

Here are eight elements we want to include in our ordinary world scene:

1. **Grab the reader's attention with a strong hook that raises questions.**
2. **Provide a goal for the hero.**
3. **Prepare the hero for heroism.**
4. **Set the physical scene with only essential details.**
5. **Begin building a bridge to the back story.**
6. **Create an emotional connection between readers and the hero.**
7. **Add anticipation and frustration to keep the connection thriving.**
8. **Establish a feeling that a crisis of some sort is coming.**

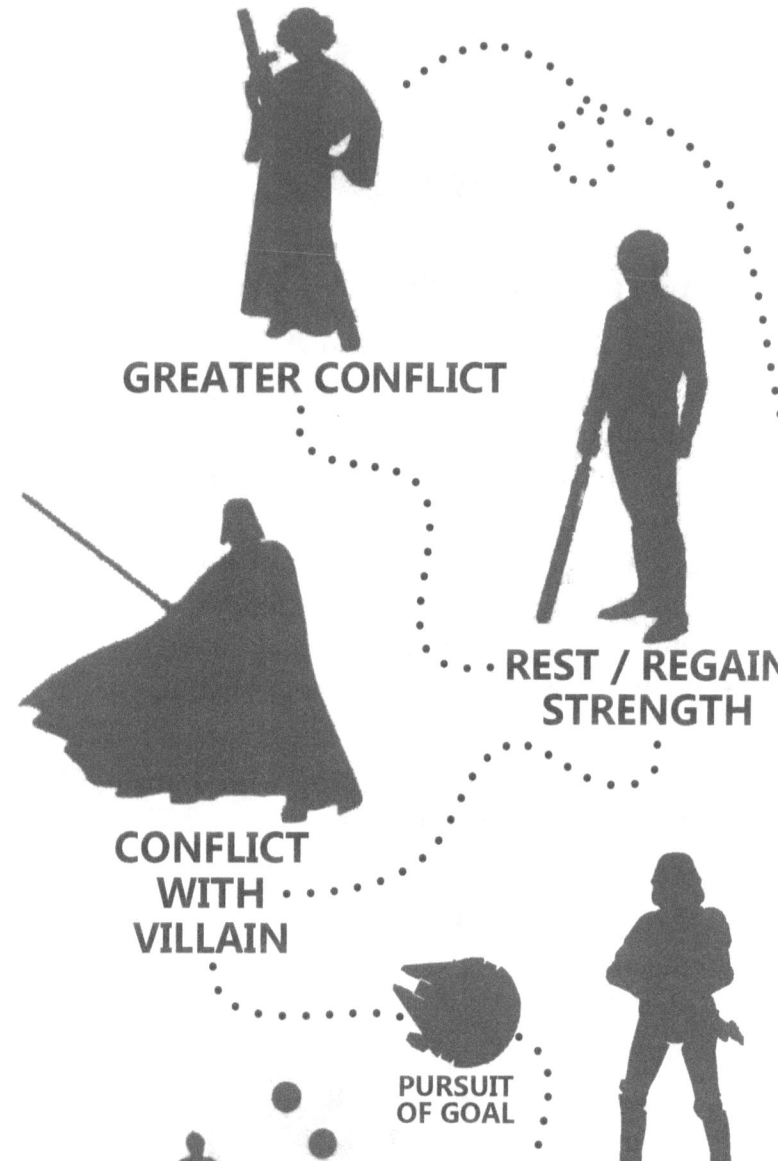

ULTIMATE CONFLICT

REST / REGAIN STRENGTH

THE GOAL

THE HERO'S JOURNEY

RESOLUTION / NEW ORDINARY WORLD

To illustrate each of these elements, I am including the beginning of my book *Reapers*.

> The death alarm sounded, that phantom punch in the gut I always dreaded. I touched the metallic gateway valve embedded in my chest at the top of my sternum—warm but not yet hot. The alarm was real. Someone in my territory would die tonight, and I had to find the poor soul. Death didn't care about the late hour. Reapers like me always stayed on call.
>
> I rose from my moth-eaten reading chair, blew out the hanging lantern's flame, and stalked across my one-room apartment to the window, guided by light from outside. The internal alarm grew stronger. Prickly vibrations raced along my cloak from the baggy sleeves to the top of the hood, tickling the two-day stubble across my cheeks and chin. Time was growing short—probably less than an hour left.
>
> I shoved open the window sash and leaned into the darkness of the urban alley. With electricity cut-off hour long past for residents, only streetlamps glowed from a neighborhood road to the left. A tall woman in a black trench coat stood at the corner holding an umbrella over her head and a suitcase at her side,

as if she were waiting for a ride, maybe a taxi.

I leaned farther out to get a better look. It hadn't rained in three days, and the skies were clear—a dry night in Chicago and too warm for a trench coat. No cabbie would pick up this woman even if he could see her.

A slight glow around her eyes confirmed her status. She was a ghost, probably level two, far too opaque to be newly dead and glowing too much to have wandered for more than a couple of weeks. If not for the death alarm, I could take the time to collect her. For now she would have to keep wandering. I had to use all my senses to figure out who was about to die.

Note how the first sentence indicates that this is the hero's ordinary world. The words "that" and "always" show that the death alarm was a regular occurrence. He is accustomed to this unpleasant alarm.

Search for ways to do the same in your story. Make it clear that the hero is in an environment to which he is accustomed, whether or not he finds this environment to be negative.

Let's see how this opening scene fulfills the eight elements for Phoenix, the heroic character in *Reapers*.

1. **Grab the reader's attention with a strong hook that raises questions.**

   In days past, readers were patient. They could endure long, detailed descriptions of settings and characters while waiting for the action to begin, maybe dozens of pages after the opening sentence. That's no longer true. We live in an instant-gratification culture. If a story doesn't grab a reader's attention after the first paragraph, maybe even the first sentence, he might put the book down and seek another, and with online previews available, this scan-and-reject process is easier than ever. Of course this isn't true of all modern readers, but it is a common trait.

   This is why I recommend that writers begin with a strong hook in the first sentence. Yet, that advice can be misinterpreted as a directive to start with intense action, such as a gunfight, a car chase, or a man hanging from a cliff with crocodiles waiting for him to fall into their open jaws.

   As exciting as you might believe such a scene to be, it will usually fall short of captivating your audience. Readers can feel lost and disconnected because they don't yet know anything about the characters or what's at stake, that is, what a character stands to lose. There is no emotional attachment that allows readers to feel the danger and sympathize with potential losses. This attachment is the crucial bond between readers and the story. Since that attachment hasn't yet taken place, the intense action can easily fall flat.

   A better option is to begin with mystery, with intrigue, with phrases that invite questions that readers want answered. In the *Reapers* example, the first sentence is, "The death alarm sounded, that phantom punch in the gut I always dreaded." The concept of a death alarm grabs attention by raising an element of mystery and prompting early questions. "What is a death alarm, and why does this character get them? How do the alarms reach him? Why does he dread the alarms?"

As readers continue, more questions come to mind. "Why does the hero have a valve embedded in his chest? Who is going to die? What is a Reaper? Why is he wearing a cloak? Why is there an electricity cut-off hour? Why is a ghost at the street? What is a level-two ghost? Are there other levels?" And I'm sure you can come up with additional questions of your own.

These questions add to the mystery of the opening scene. As long as we feed readers answers to some questions while keeping some unanswered, readers will continue turning the pages to satisfy the thirst for more.

Writers should delay intense action for at least a few paragraphs or pages until readers have a chance to connect. First show some of the hero's character qualities. Allow readers to understand what's at stake so that intense action has purpose in readers' minds and a potential sense of loss if the character suffers defeat.

Here is another example, the beginning of *Precisely Terminated* by my daughter Amanda L. Davis.

> How nice it must be to sleep so peacefully when doom awaited at dawn. Letting out a sigh, Faye pulled a threadbare blanket from a top bunk and surveyed the many

beds and sleeping bodies lined up in the cramped room. How little they all knew, these poor, ignorant laborers. Perhaps they would die unaware of the tragedy about to befall them.

As she folded the blanket and laid it back on the bed, a tear welled in her eye. Why did it have to happen this way? She was only a nursemaid, one slave in the midst of thousands. Why should she die because of one man's actions? It simply wasn't fair. No, it was cruel, inhumane, tragic ... evil.

She slowly clenched a fist. Fair or unfair, the time had come. The plan had to proceed.

Take note of the hook beginning, the statement that doom awaited at dawn. Readers will immediately wonder what that doom might be. Then comes an opportunity to get to know a character as Faye goes about her business in her ordinary world. She is a nursemaid, which means that taking care of a bed is to be expected.

More questions come to mind. Who is the one man? What were his actions? What is the plan that has to proceed? Why does she know that doom is coming and apparently no one else knows? Why isn't she telling the others by sounding an alarm?

The hook is set without any intense action, and readers want to know the answers to their questions, especially what happens next. They will read more.

2. Provide a goal for the hero.

Let's go back to *Reapers*. "Someone in my territory would die tonight, and I had to find the poor soul." Exploring the hero's ordinary world is more interesting if the character has something important to do, in this case, to find who was going to die. He might accomplish this goal early in the story, or he might fail, and then we will replace that goal with a bigger one, which I will explain in detail in a later section.

The best goals are related to the hero's ordinary world, something he would normally do. This Reaper collects souls, so it's not unusual for him to have this goal in the opening scene. Such a goal allows the hero to use skills that he often employs, thereby letting readers know what his abilities are. This way, readers will learn the hero's boundaries—what he can do against future obstacles as well as what he lacks.

If the hero is a student, maybe he has to pass a crucial test. Maybe an athlete is training for a big game. A mother has a sick child, and she is seeking medical help. An entrepreneur's new business is opening soon, and he is getting ready for the launch. These goals are all within a character's ordinary world, and they give that character something significant to do.

When readers understand the hero's goal, they enjoy following him through a series of actions. They cheer the hero toward that end. They feel the tension when an obstacle or potential failure approaches. They understand what's at stake. They sense the pain of loss if the hero fails.

Without a known goal, the action feels like aimless wandering, and any character traits we are trying to develop or back story elements we are trying to explore result in a tedious experience for readers. In short, the opening is boring.

In *Precisely Terminated*, Faye has an early goal, to help the plan proceed, whatever that is, and readers learn about the plan in the next few paragraphs. They also meet the "one man" whose actions brought the doom about, which answers one of the questions that the opening raised.

The following pattern takes shape—Raise questions. Provide traits that connect readers to the hero as he tries to achieve a goal. Answer one or more of the questions. Raise more questions. Repeat.

This cycle will keep readers turning the pages.

3. Prepare the hero for heroism.

The best heroes are the unlikely ones. Few people would suspect that these characters could rise to become champions against all odds, perhaps especially the people readers meet in the hero's ordinary world.

One hero might be small of stature, like a hobbit from the Shire. Another might be young and inexperienced, like a farm hand named Luke Skywalker. Another might be a little girl from a war-torn nation, like Lucy Pevensie in the Narnia tales.

Then, when the characters triumph over seemingly insurmountable obstacles, readers rejoice, because, in the privacy of their quiet nooks, they might perceive similar obstacles in their own lives, and they, too, would need to rise above expectations to overcome the Orcs, Death Stars, and White Witches of their worlds. They long to be heroes themselves, as unlikely as that dream might seem to others.

For an unlikely hero to come across as realistic, we need to prepare our heroic character in the following ways.

- **He should be likeable and possess inner virtue.**
- **His motivations to act should be clear and praiseworthy.**
- **He should have weaknesses that make his objective seem unlikely.**

Let's see how each of these items work in a story.

He should be likeable and possess inner virtue.

For the Hero's Journey structure to be successful, the hero needs to be a character readers want to encourage. Therefore, he should have one or more qualities readers can admire.

In the *Reapers* example, notice the following: "Reapers like me always stayed on call." From this statement we see that the hero is dedicated, a positive quality.

"She was a ghost, probably level two, far too opaque to be newly dead and glowing too much to have wandered for more than a couple of weeks." His ability to detect these characteristics by watching from a distance proves that he is skilled and experienced.

"I had to use all my senses to figure out who was about to die." He is passionate about completing his goal. He likely has empathy for the dying person.

Readers conclude that the hero is a decent person. Then, as the story continues and the hero makes sacrifices for others, that positive perception will strengthen.

His motivations to act should be clear and praiseworthy.

Since we want readers to cheer for the hero, the reasons for his choices have to be understandable, and readers need to view the motivations as good and noble, or at least neutral and not immoral or hurtful to others. If he is selfish and his goals seem to be centered on himself alone, readers won't easily attach, and they might give up on him early on.

He should have weaknesses that make his objective seem unlikely.

It's important to show at least one weakness in the hero. This way, readers can watch him grow as a result of the challenges and suffering that the journey will bring. Also, the hero's flaws should give readers the idea that his battles might be impossible to win. This makes the final triumph that much sweeter.

These flaws should be deficiencies in maturity, wisdom, experience, or skill rather than moral flaws. If the hero is immoral, it is more difficult for readers to believe that he would be willing to endure the sacrificial suffering that is typical of such journeys, since immoral people usually lack selfless motivations and are guided by self-pleasing drives rather than altruistic ideals.

Redemption stories, on the other hand, often include characters who start out immoral and learn a better way, but that's a different story structure, not a hero's journey. Also, anti-hero stories follow the adventures of characters who might have many flaws that can be truly disturbing or even evil, and authors might try to put them in a hero's journey. Obviously they are free to do so, but they are less realistic as heroes, and, as I noted earlier, readers will have a more difficult time attaching to them.

Since flaws that come from lack of experience, wisdom, or skill are nearly universal, readers can relate, and they will excuse the hero's flaws as something everyone encounters and cheer for him.

For example, in *Reapers:*

> I rose from my moth-eaten reading chair, blew out the hanging lantern's flame, and stalked across my one-room apartment to the window, guided by light from outside."

Since the hero notices the bad condition of his chair, it's likely that he is not satisfied with his environment. The verb "stalked" (and later "shoved") indicates possible anger. Although he is dedicated, he probably doesn't like his job, which can be interpreted as a flaw.

Later, readers learn that the hero is somewhat blind to the real causes of the troubles that plague his city. He is too focused on the trees, if you will, and cannot see the forest. He is also a loner who has a hard time trusting new friends. These are flaws, but they are not moral failings, and readers will easily forgive him, understanding that his difficult circumstances have birthed these negative traits, and they will enjoy watching his suffering rub away those rough edges.

4. Set the physical scene with only essential details.

At the beginning of the story, we are trying to hook readers in a way that will keep the pages turning. On the first page, readers likely aren't interested in physical-setting details, such as textures, colors, how furniture is arranged, or how many bulbs are in a light fixture. Yet, we need to provide enough images for readers to paint the essential mental picture.

We do this by employing the following methods:

- **Place the scene in a relatively familiar setting.**

- **Use "quality" words to paint the scene rather than a quantity of words.**

- **Describe items that are unusual for your setting or details that act as foreshadowing.**

- **Have the hero interact with one or more of these items.**

Let's look at the *Reapers* example again to illustrate these methods.

Place the scene in a relatively familiar setting.

Notice this phrase - "stalked across my one-room apartment to the window." Stating that this is a one-room apartment provides an immediate mental picture. The reader's image might not match the author's exactly, but accuracy isn't important at this stage.

You might use a school classroom, a library, a spaceship cabin (readers have seen them in movies), a forest, or a museum. Once you mention one of these labels, readers will paint an initial image with their own understanding of what the scene looks like and then fill it in with the details you provide, however few they might be.

Use quality words to paint the scene rather than a quantity of words.

In *Reapers*, "moth-eaten reading chair" indicates that this apartment might be dingy or in poor repair, which makes readers imagine such a room. In their mental picture, maybe paint is peeling from the walls, a faucet leaks, or bare spots in the carpet expose worn wood. Whether or not a reader is correct doesn't matter, because these details aren't crucial to your story. Yet, a mental setting of some kind is crucial, that is, an imagined stage for the characters to act upon, and later phrases allow the images to develop.

Also, "leaned into the darkness of the urban alley" paints a picture of the outside setting. There was no need to mention trash cans, graffiti on walls, or scurrying rats, because readers drew them in. Again, these details don't matter, so you shouldn't write about them yet, because this is the time to hook readers, not drown them with details. Let the reader paint these pictures as they are inspired by your high-quality words.

Describe items that are unusual for your setting or details that act as foreshadowing.

As the author of your story, you know ahead of time (or find out later as you write the story) which details are important in your opening scene. You should mention those details in order to clarify the setting or foreshadow later events.

Foreshadowing is a writing device in which we give a clue that something might occur in the future. We want to show weapons, character abilities, and just about any other significant story element in an inactive state before it becomes active.

For example, we want to show a sword in the scabbard at a warrior's hip before he draws it in battle. Otherwise, it seems to come out of nowhere and surprises readers. I have much more information on foreshadowing in the toolbox section on page 192.

In the *Reapers* example, "the hanging lantern's flame" is such a foreshadowing detail. I included it because the lantern is unusual in an apartment setting, and it provides foreshadowing that the city residents have no electricity after a certain hour.

I also included the following two details:

"I touched the metallic gateway valve embedded in my chest at the top of my sternum." Since this valve is a crucial difference between a Reaper and a normal human, I wanted to show it as early as possible, that Reapers have this burden to bear.

"Prickly vibrations raced along my cloak from the baggy sleeves to the top of the hood, tickling the two-day stubble across my cheeks and chin." The cloak is a crucial element in the story that I used constantly, giving me reason to describe it right away. Also, I mentioned the stubble to give away the hero's gender. Before that point, the character could have been male or female in a reader's mind.

Have the hero interact with one or more of these items.

In *Reapers*, notice that the hero blows out the flame, touches the valve, leans out into the alley, and feels the prickly vibrations. Each detail comes to life as the character experiences it, as if he is guiding readers through the scene. Simply describing the details as if the scene were a still-life painting halts the action and raises the risk of boredom. Keep the story going, and readers will feel as if they are experiencing the surroundings along with the character in real time.

If you're describing a castle, don't merely say that it has two turrets and a drawbridge. Show the character skulking through the shadow cast by the two turrets and stepping on the creaking drawbridge. Don't say that the grass blades in the field are knee high. Show the grass blades whipping the character's knees as he dashes across the field.

This kind of interaction, however, is not always possible. Your character might be chained to a dungeon wall, which keeps him from petting the rat that's crawling along the floor. Still, you can show the rat moving, which makes the scene stay alive. Show leaves rustling on a tree, a bird in flight, or a stone tumbling down a slope. As characters witness these details in motion, readers are witnessing them at the same time, and they feel like they are with the characters in the scene.

I will provide more details on this topic when I discuss intimate point of view in the toolbox section, beginning on page 107.

5. Begin building a bridge to the back story.

Every story has a back story, that is, events that occurred before the opening line. When your story begins, the preceding events are a mystery to readers, some of which readers need to know in order to fully understand the main story.

Many writers choose to begin the story at an intriguing point in time in order to hook readers, then they proceed to fill in the back story by dumping a load of information all at once. This method halts the main story and frustrates readers. They wonder, "What happened to the intriguing part? I want to read what happens next. I don't care about the stuff in the past."

Halting the main story in order to dump back story is like breaking a promise. The author baited readers with intrigue, then threw the story back to another time and/or place. If the back story is so important that the author has to provide the details all at once, then he should have started the story at an earlier point in time.

A better option is to begin the story in the hero's ordinary world right before a crisis event (to be explained in detail later), and provide clues to the back story while continuing the main story. We insert these clues one by one, and readers collect them and mentally put them together to re-create the back story, like bricks that build a bridge to past events as well as the characters' backgrounds.

In the *Reapers* example, the early back story clues are subtle. "Someone in my territory" indicates that the hero has a territory to oversee. The city is divided into sections. Why? Later clues will provide the answer.

"I could take the time to collect her" indicates that Reapers have a feeling of responsibility to collect ghosts. Readers then understand that this is likely part of a Reaper's duties, though they don't yet know why.

As the story progresses, we provide more and more clues until readers are able to put them all together. This is hard work, much harder than simply dumping all of the information at once, but it is better storytelling.

One of the difficulties we encounter is how to provide clues in a subtle fashion without creating contrivances, that is, clues that seem forced into the text for the sole purpose of providing readers with information.

Some writers create a conversation between characters, and the dialogue provides the back-story information. This is called dialogue dumping, and it halts a story in its tracks just as surely as a narrative dumping of facts. It can also look much worse to readers, because such dialogue usually comes across as forced and unnatural.

For example:

> "Your battle armor looks splendid, my king," Sir John said. "It reminds me of the previous war in which you won a great victory over the Wolfkin and established our expanded borders."
>
> The king nodded. "Indeed. Because of that conquest, I am now sovereign over the seven species of sentient creatures.

We are at peace with all but the Wolfkin, and now we go to ensure that the border stays where it is."

This is an ugly example of contrived dialogue that attempts to inform readers of back story elements. These two men would never have this discussion, because they both already know these facts.

Of course, this is an extreme example, but I hope you can see the principle. Try to avoid dialogue that is information driven and would not be spoken under the circumstances.

Good back-story bridge building includes providing hints that come across as natural and non-intrusive. Readers pick up on them almost without thinking, and the bricks come together without effort and without halting the main story.

I am often asked about providing back-story elements in a prologue. I advise against prologues in most cases because many readers will skip over them and start in chapter one. If the information you want to include in a prologue is essential to understanding your story, then it's likely that more than half of your readers will bypass it and miss the essential information.

If you must dump essential back story information, label it chapter one. Then readers won't skip it. Still, it's better to carefully put in small bits of those elements into the main story a little at a time. Again, it's hard work, but it's worth it.

Although some of my novels have a prologue, if I had them to do over again, I would put that information in chapter one in all but two cases—Eye of the Oracle and Song of the Ovulum. Those prologues are short, and I wrote them as personal communications between a character and the readers, a different style from the rest of the book. Those two aspects make the material ill-suited for inclusion in chapter one, yet acceptable in a prologue.

6. **Create an emotional connection between readers and the hero.**

Creating an emotional connection between readers and characters is a crucial goal. Readers must be able to relate on a heart level with the people they read about. We do this by forcing the characters to deal with issues readers can relate with, and we do so as early in the story as possible.

At the beginning, try to show the negative emotions your hero is experiencing, maybe one or more from the following list:

- Loss
- Sadness
- Loneliness
- Suffering
- Injustice
- Heartbreak
- Betrayal
- Dissatisfaction
- Withdrawal/Numbness

Your readers have experienced many of these emotions themselves. They know how much pain they can bring. As readers sympathize, they want the hero to find comfort and a way to resolve the issues that are causing the pain. In short, they feel sorry for the hero.

Even in the midst of the hero's woes, also show his determination to overcome so that he doesn't appear to be pitiful. We want heroes who are in difficult circumstances but are making the best of it anyway. These are qualities readers will connect with.

Here are some issues I try to include in order to show the hero's difficulties:

- **Physical need – A common handicap, illness, or negative physical environment.**
- **Emotional issue – A need or desire that most readers have felt.**
- **A purpose – A goal that most readers would find praiseworthy.**
- **Urgency – The goal must be gained soon.**
- **Obstacles – Barriers that readers would identify with.**
- **Vulnerability – A soft spot to exploit.**
- **Sacrifice – The hero performs a sacrificial act to overcome obstacles.**

Here are examples from the opening of *Reapers*, quoted again with boldfaced highlights.

> The death alarm sounded, that **phantom punch in the gut** I always dreaded. I touched the metallic gateway valve embedded in my chest at the top of my sternum—warm but not yet hot. The alarm was real. Someone in my territory

would die tonight, and **I had to find the poor soul**. Death didn't care about **the late hour**. Reapers like me always stayed on call.

I rose from my **moth-eaten reading chair**, blew out the hanging lantern's flame, and stalked across my one-room apartment to the window, guided by light from outside. The internal alarm grew stronger. Prickly vibrations raced along my cloak from the baggy sleeves to the top of the hood, tickling the two-day stubble across my cheeks and chin. Time was growing short—**probably less than an hour left.**

Let's look at the categories of the bold-faced phrases.

Phantom punch in the gut - an emotional reaction to bad news. Most people have felt that kind of punch.

I had to find the poor soul - a purpose that readers will cheer for. The word *poor* shows the character's concern, and this will be transmitted to readers.

The late hour - an obstacle that will increase the goal's difficultly, making readers wonder how he will overcome it. Readers will want to ride along and witness the effort to see if it will succeed or fail.

Moth-eaten reading chair - a negative physical environment that will create sympathy. Most readers are more likely to cheer for a poor man than for a rich one.

Probably less than an hour left – urgency that will encourage readers to be concerned.

I employed five of these emotional-attachment tools within the flow of the story. My hope was to generate an immediate connection, because once such a connection is firmly established, it will last throughout the story.

For more examples, let's continue with the next three paragraphs from *Reapers*.

> I shoved open the window sash and leaned into the darkness of the urban alley. With **electricity cut-off hour long past for residents**, only streetlamps glowed from a neighborhood road to the left. A tall woman in a black trench coat stood at the corner holding an umbrella over her head and a suitcase at her side, as if she were waiting for a ride, maybe a taxi.
>
> I leaned farther out to get a better look. It hadn't rained in three days, and the skies were clear—a dry night in Chicago and too warm for a trench coat. **No cabbie would pick up this woman even if he could see her.**
>
> A slight glow around her eyes confirmed her status. She was a ghost, probably level two, far too opaque to be newly dead and glowing too much to have wandered for more than a couple of weeks. **If not for the death alarm, I**

could take the time to collect her. For now she would have to keep wandering. **I had to use all my senses to figure out who was about to die.**

Electricity cut-off hour long past for residents - a negative environment.

No cabbie would pick up this woman even if he could see her - emotional issue—the hero's desire to help.

If not for the death alarm, I could take the time to collect her - urgency.

I had to use all my senses to figure out who was about to die - a purpose.

Although I employed these tools early and created an emotional connection, I didn't drop the tools later. It's important to continue this process so readers will stay on board and continue sympathizing with the hero, but the frequency of using these tools can decrease.

Now let's focus on a couple of these methods.

Vulnerability - A soft spot to exploit.

Every hero needs a tender spot in both body and heart. Even Superman had both—Kryptonite and Lois Lane. I like to reveal a vulnerability early for two reasons. (1) When the villain exploits the vulnerability, it isn't a surprise, as if the issue were tacked on late in the game. (2) The vulnerability is an aspect the reader can wonder and worry about as the story progresses. Even worry is part of emotionally connecting.

Here is how I did this in *Reapers*:

> On the dresser's top, I slid a tri-fold picture frame closer and ran a finger along the photos of my father, mother, and Misty. I touched her image. Misty. The girl across the street. The girl I had known all my life before I had to leave for good.
>
> I touched the pewter band on my ring finger, a gift from Misty when we were both thirteen, the day we confirmed our promise to each other—the day I left home for the last time.
>
> Her voice, flavored as always with a lovely Scottish accent, filtered into my mind. "Twenty years is a long time," she had whispered as she rested her head on my shoulder. "No matter what, I'll be waiting for you. Just promise me you'll do everything you can to get out early. I hear there are shortcuts."
>
> I pushed the frame back in place. Someday I would see her again ... if she was still alive.

Misty, a lost love, is Phoenix's soft spot, and readers feel his love and concern for her. As you might expect, I used the soft spot later to stab his soul. Experienced readers know ahead of time that such a stab will come, and they will worry about it, not knowing when it will come or how it will manifest.

Sacrifice – Hero performs a sacrificial act to overcome obstacles.

Readers like to cheer for sacrificial heroes. In order to establish that quality, show a sacrificial act early. Make the act small at first, then build up to bigger sacrifices so that each step isn't a huge surprise but rather a reader-pleasing event that grows and grows.

Here is an early sacrifice for Phoenix in *Reapers*:

> I shook the bottle, making it rattle. "Only two pills left. If they don't help, I brought something injectable, but it's way past expired so it has to be a last resort."
>
> "We believe in you, Phoenix," Colm said. "You will make the right choice."
>
> "Let's just hope a DEO doesn't show up, or all choices are out the door. Word on the street says that Molly's critical, so an officer might get wind of it."

Readers learn elsewhere in the story that medicine smuggling carried the death penalty. Therefore, Phoenix acted sacrificially to bring the pills to help the family. The odds that he would get caught were high enough to worry about, but he didn't yet have a gun to his head, so this initial sacrifice wasn't huge. Readers can identify with a first reasonable risk, and they won't be shocked as he risks more and more with each future sacrifice. They will also appreciate each faithful step as the hero grows and excels.

7. Add anticipation and frustration to keep the connection thriving.

Once an emotional connection is established, it's important to keep the connection alive as the action continues through the opening scene. We do this by adding anticipation and frustration, factors that make readers anxious about the hero. Here are some anxiety-inducing devices.

- **Pauses**
- **First attempt never works.**
- **Obstacles increase.**
- **Complete failure achieving early goal.**
- **Failure leads to a bigger goal.**
- **Increasing sacrifice.**

Let's look at each of these in turn.

Pauses – A pause immediately before an attempt to achieve a goal reminds readers of the importance of the goal, thereby enhancing anticipation. If possible, restate the goal and the danger.

Readers enjoy action and anticipate it. A great way to heighten the enjoyment is to include a pause immediately before an action sequence. During a pause, remind readers of the goal and potential obstacles that could result in danger.

Here is an example from *Reapers*:

> I returned the flashlight to the belt and pulled my hood over my head far enough to shade my eyes. I had to display the persona. To the dying and the

bereaved, confidence in my abilities meant everything.

I patted my cloak pocket where the pill bottle and syringe lay. Communicating my hope to cure instead of collect would be tricky. As Crandyke said, the Council's spies could be anywhere, even in the midst of a close-knit family.

"To the dying and the bereaved" reminds readers of why the hero is where he is. The presence of the pill bottle is a reminder that he is taking a risk, smuggling medicine. The idea that spies might be watching adds a potential obstacle.

With these ideas firmly planted in readers' minds, the coming action sequence will be enhanced, because readers will expect danger to arise and understand what's at stake. We include reminders immediately before the action, because readers might have forgotten or not noticed clues that we dropped here and there in earlier parts of the story, and it's natural for the hero to consider these ideas while he anticipates his next move. This method is like an injection of adrenaline to make the pages turn.

First attempt never works – Avoid allowing a goal to be achieved on the first attempt. The success will be too easy and less satisfying.

We always appreciate accomplishments that are hard to achieve much more than those that come easily. The same is true with regard to story characters. If the first attempt at achieving a goal succeeds, then the goal was too easy, and readers yawn and think, "Ho hum."

Let the first attempt fail, and maybe two or three attempts. In fact, the plan to attain the goal can end in disaster.

From *Reapers*:

> Molly choked on the pills and coughed them up. Her body stiffened, and she let out a moan. While the three patted her hands and stroked her head in futility, I swallowed hard. Even after more than three years as a Reaper, the sight of a dying child still tore a hole in my heart.
>
> My cloak vibrated, sending hot prickles across my arms. The end was near. Only one hope remained—the syringe.

Phoenix tried the pills, but they didn't work. This is a small failure, but it is a real one. If you read the story, you will see that other attempts fail as well, and the hero is unable to achieve his goal.

Failure ratchets up the tension, because it shows readers that failure is possible or even likely. Readers won't know if the hero will achieve future goals that might be far more important. This keeps readers in suspense.

Obstacles Increase – New obstacles add frustration, which will enhance relief and the sense of triumph later. We can all relate to frustration.

As the hero attempts to achieve goals, we must build obstacles. As I mentioned earlier, an easily achieved goal provides less satisfaction, and, as you might expect, a goal that is achieved after great toil provides a massive amount of satisfaction. Therefore, set obstacles in the character's path—big obstacles and plenty of them.

Toil produces suffering and frustration, and these two factors are keys to maintaining an emotional connection with readers. We continue to connect to readers' hearts through portrayals of negative emotions.

Why? Because, as I mentioned earlier, most readers have suffered through emotional turmoil themselves, and they want to reach out and connect with characters who suffer in the same way. Readers want to see how characters react to the obstacles, how they face the difficulties, and how they overcome.

These examples encourage many readers to face and overcome their own obstacles, which is one of the main reasons authors pick up the proverbial pen. We hope to inspire readers and improve their lives in some way, even if it's simply emotional encouragement.

In *Reapers*, Phoenix has been unable to help Molly with the pills he smuggled. Then a bigger obstacle enters, a Death Enforcement Officer who arrives to make sure Molly dies:

> As I reached into my pocket, the rusty hinges at the front door squeaked. Everyone froze. Fiona whispered, "I heard no knock."
>
> Colm shoved the pill bottle into his pocket. Fiona and Colleen rose and backed away from the bed, their eyes

wide with fear. Molly's body loosened, and she breathed in gasping spasms.

The bedroom door swung open. A tall woman dressed in black leather stepped in and scanned the room. Piercing gray eyes set beneath a somber brow gave her the aspect of a bird of prey searching for a victim. With youthful face, trim body, and blonde hair draped over her shoulders, she looked nothing like the steroid-jacked male officer who normally patrolled at night. Yet, the leather pants and jacket with a Gateway insignia on the left breast pocket confirmed her status as a death officer of some kind.

Her shifting gaze halted at Molly. "A young one," she said in a low monotone. "My condolences."

The situation was already bad enough, but now it is suddenly much worse. Emotions are heightened. What will Phoenix do? How can he save Molly?

Notice that I made sure Phoenix identified this woman as a death officer as soon as possible. That designation is crucial for building the tension. If not for that, readers wouldn't know that her appearance means big trouble for Phoenix and the suffering family.

Complete failure achieving early goal – An early goal should not be the most important one, though failure in the early goal causes real pain. Let failure happen.

As I mentioned earlier, when the hero fails to achieve an early goal, this proves that failure is always possible, maybe even probable, even with the big goals, thereby enhancing the danger and suspense as the story progresses. Also, since everyone experiences failure at times, readers can relate, and they will be in true suspense as they wonder if failure will occur:

Here is how it works in *Reapers*:

> Molly's eyes opened. She blinked at Alex, then at her family. She smiled weakly for a moment, whispered an almost imperceptible "I love you," then closed her eyes and fell limp. Her head lolled to the side, and she breathed no more.
>
> Fiona sobbed. Colm pulled her close and stroked her back. Colleen just stared, her mouth hanging open.
>
> Her eyes still flickering, Alex rose and backed away from the bed. "Reaper ... her soul awaits."

Molly died. A little girl passed away in spite of the hero's attempts to save her. Since readers can relate, the emotional connection is secure, and they will keep turning the pages, truly not knowing if the hero will succeed as he attempts to achieve the next goal.

Failure leads to a bigger goal – If the hero fails, make the failure a stepping stone to something more important.

One of the intriguing qualities of failure is that it can create a goal that is more urgent than the previous one. It is through failure that we come face to face with our weaknesses and need for improvement, and failure often creates a new crisis that inspires a bigger goal.

In *Reapers*, Phoenix's initial goal was to save Molly. He failed. One of the results of his failure is that Molly's family members are arrested and taken to the dreaded corrections camp. He also gains help from a Reaper friend named Sing, short for Singapore.

> I crept to the front of Colm's house, Sing following, and leaned over the edge of the roof. At the entry steps, the door opened, and Alex's voice rose from below.
>
> "Pack one small suitcase for each member of your family. The bus will come for you soon, so get ready quickly. And don't try to escape. I already have someone watching your house."
>
> "Bus?" Sing whispered.
>
> "A camp bus. She's sending them to corrections." I heaved a sigh. "I guess I don't have any choice. I shouldn't have left them alone with her in the first place."

Now Phoenix has more people to save, several innocent lives instead of one. This bigger goal and elevated urgency will keep the pages turning.

Increasing sacrifice – The hero willingly exposes himself to danger, whether physical or emotional, and the danger increases.

A bigger goal and more urgency are helpful in increasing intensity, but the new goal must also require greater sacrifices from the hero.

Since sacrifice naturally includes suffering, be sure to make your hero suffer more. Each time you create a bigger goal, increase the sacrificial suffering to match it.

In *Reapers*, take a look at how the new goal's danger manifests itself as Phoenix has a discussion with Alex about coming to the corrections camp.

> Alex shot to her feet. She grabbed my arm, bent it behind my back, and shoved me against the wall, rubbing my cheek on the rough plaster. Cold steel pressed against my skull. Her breaths blew past my ear, hot and heavy. "You think you're so smart, don't you? Three years on the street, and you know it all. You think you're bucking the system being Mr. Nice Guy Reaper, looking down your nose at loyalists. You think I'm just an enforcer who gets her jollies inflicting pain." She twisted my arm, sending shock waves to my spine. "Well, you're wrong. There is method to my madness. Pain is just one

tool in my arsenal of ways to get what I want. And what I want right now is for you to realize that you're dealing with someone who could jerk your soul out of your skull and hurl you into the abyss without a second thought. And if I find out you've been lying to me, that's exactly what I'll do."

I grimaced but refused to grunt. "What's the abyss?"

"A place no one wants to go." She spun me around and pressed the gun barrel between my eyes. "You have nothing to worry about if you'll keep that smart-aleck mouth of yours shut."

The abyss is a new danger, a place Phoenix knows nothing about other than Alex's warning that no one wants to go there. Just the word *abyss* conjures frightening images, and readers know that Phoenix will have to eventually face this peril. In so doing, he will have to make greater sacrifices in order to overcome the danger.

8. Establish a feeling that a crisis of some sort is coming.

The hero's journey cannot begin unless the hero leaves his ordinary world, whether the departure and journey are physical, mental, emotional, or spiritual. A crisis needs to take place that creates a goal, a much bigger goal than we established in the opening scene, and the new goal will serve as motivation for the hero to start and complete the journey.

Sometimes a hero's ordinary world can be a boring existence, both to the hero and to readers. In such cases, the author needs to foreshadow that a crisis is coming, an inciting incident that will change everything. Although the hero's everyday actions might still be mundane, the impending danger keeps interest high.

Here are some ways to let readers know that a crisis event is coming:

- **Foreboding Language**
- **A Promise of Action**
- **Potential Dangers Along the Way**
- **New Questions Arise**
- **Real Dangers Activate**

Let's see how to use these methods.

Foreboding Language - Words and phrases that feel dark and scary, that provoke fears or frustrations.

Look again at the initial *Reapers* excerpt on page 8. Take note of some of the foreboding verbiage from the beginning: The death alarm. Phantom punch. Dreaded. The poor soul. Death didn't care. Stalked across. Prickly vibrations. Shoved open. All of these examples are dark, worrisome phrases or strong reactions to deep-seated feelings. They prompt readers to conjure dark thoughts about the future. Readers know something bad will soon happen that will drastically affect the hero.

A Promise of Action - An indication that a critical event is coming soon.

In the opening excerpt, I ended with "I had to use all my senses to figure out who was about to die."

This tells readers a simple fact: the hero is going to do something important soon. Readers expect this action and look forward to it. Experienced readers realize that this early goal will likely alter the hero's present course.

Precisely Terminated has the same kind of promise. Go back to the excerpt on page 11. Notice that it ends with "The plan had to proceed." Readers believe that turning the page will reveal the plan, whatever that is, and the action will intensify. Danger is right around the corner.

Potential Dangers Along the Way - As the hero prepares to try to achieve the early goal in his ordinary world, mention at least one of the dangers he might face.

Potential danger builds tension that something dangerous will certainly happen. Notice three potential dangers mentioned in this excerpt from Reapers.

> "Right. Your first cycle." I glanced along the trash-cluttered alleyway below. Still no messenger. With bandits abundant lately, a messenger likely wouldn't venture out until the last minute. "How many souls do you have?"
>
> "Not enough." She leaned into the light, revealing the whites of her eyes, a stark contrast against her skin's lovely dark tone, a hue resembling coffee with a shot of cream, quite different from my cream-only complexion, though her hair color matched mine—darker brown than her

skin. "If I meet quota by morning," she said, "will you take me with you?"

"If you knew what the Gateway extraction feels like, you wouldn't be so anxious to go."

"A Reaper has to learn sometime, and I'd rather go with someone who knows the ropes."

"Fair enough." I wrinkled my brow. "Are you going to the executions to make quota? Do you have any idea how dangerous it is?"

"You go reap Molly. I can handle a little danger."

The three dangers are bandits, a difficult extraction, and the happenings at executions. Tension mounts as readers wonder if the hero will face these dangers as he proceeds to "figure out who was about to die."

New Questions Arise - The hero's actions should raise new questions paragraph after paragraph.

When we raise more and more questions, readers will contemplate them along with the hero. How will the hero meet his challenges? What happens at executions? Who is being executed? What happens during an extraction? Do bandits steal souls?

As we learned early on, questions that need answers are a driving force behind the turning of pages. As we answer these questions for readers, we need to add more.

Real Dangers Activate - The hero sees a threat of real danger, not just a potential one. He might not have to confront it yet, but it is clear that it is near and could soon be upon him.

Notice the new questions and active danger as *Reapers* continues:

> She thrust herself off the rail and dropped, plunging through the brighter light. With her shimmering black cloak fanned out, she looked like a glowing raven sailing toward the pavement, though sepia curls lifting above her head spoiled the image.
>
> She landed, bending her knees to absorb the impact, and ran toward the alley opening. The ghost at the corner stood nearby, but Sing paid no attention as she breezed past and slinked into the shadows—a sable cat, stealthy and sleek.
>
> I leaned out again. Why didn't she try to collect the ghost? As a rookie, maybe she thought she wasn't experienced enough to handle such a difficult reaping.
>
> A motorcycle rumbled to life in the direction Sing had run, and the sound slowly drifted away. That could mean trouble—a Death Enforcement Officer

had probably spotted Sing and was now tailing her. These DEOs couldn't stand to let a death go by without harassing a Reaper and tracking every soul's progress through the Gateway.

I didn't have time to worry about Sing. She would have to handle her own troubles.

Again new questions arise. Phoenix wonders about his new acquaintance, Sing. What is she all about? Why didn't she act in an expected manner? When the hero contemplates these questions, the reader will do so as well, and the mystery will add to the feeling that something big is about to occur.

And a real danger activates. The motorcycle following Sing is a real threat, not just a worry. Such a danger is a promise to readers that someone will soon be in trouble.

Keep repeating this cycle of adding questions and dangers. Even if a hero's ordinary world seems boring on a superficial level, you can spice it up with foreshadowing that something big and perhaps dangerous is about to occur. Do this by adding Foreboding Language, A Promise of Action, Potential Dangers, New Questions, and Real Dangers. These elements will keep readers turning the pages.

Summary of the Ordinary World

The hero needs a goal to achieve in the opening scene, something associated with his ordinary world, whether the goal is big or small. Then we allow the hero to fail, which is a crucial step in developing the character's qualities as he reacts to the failure.

This reaction defines his current state of mind and inner heart. It's a baseline that allows the hero to reveal what he is made of, and readers will be interested in seeing how the hero changes during the story.

Failure in achieving the initial goal often leads to the crisis event. The crisis event creates a new goal, and this goal is often the story's big goal, sometimes called the object of desire, which drives the hero forward for the rest of the tale.

Phoenix's new goal is created by the crisis, birthed by his failure. After losing Molly, he needs to rescue her family from the corrections camp, and this becomes a longer-term goal, which is not part of his ordinary world. This is new and different, and it forces him to leave his normal life.

While in his ordinary world, he was satisfied with performing his duties and occasionally violating protocol in order to offer help. Yet, he did not try to break the system that created the death and misery around him. He thought himself incapable of such a huge task.

Because of the crisis, he is pushed harder to do more than his customary duties. He now must challenge the death-industry system itself, though his next goal is still smaller than breaking the entire system. He just wants to rescue this family. And, as you might expect, he will learn that rescuing the family will require challenging the system as he faithfully pursues the goal that the crisis created.

This concludes the Ordinary World element of the Hero's Journey structure. As is true with much of my writing advice, starting your story this way is not a rule written on a tablet of stone. Other starting points are valid.

For example, you can start after the crisis and have readers meet the hero during the pursuit of the goal. This often works when the hero's pursuit is long and laborious and has become a new ordinary world for him. The crisis created this environment, and it is often an awful existence, which provokes readers to hope for success.

Although that option can work quite well, I recommend that writers master the traditional hero's journey structure before attempting a story that deviates from it.

Once you gain experience in how and why the structure works so well, you will be able to tweak any aspect of the structure and still absorb readers in your story, because you will know what creates intrigue and what destroys it, what establishes emotional connections and what breaks them, and, most important, what places readers in the journey and what forces them out.

The Crisis

Let's begin with a list of crisis characteristics.

1. **The crisis is a terrible event that destroys the hero's ordinary world.**
2. **The crisis creates a goal, the objective of the story.**
3. **Achieving the desired goal is dangerous.**
4. **Motivation to achieve the goal must be strong, both externally and internally.**

Now we'll look at how each of these works in a story.

1. **The crisis is a terrible event that destroys the hero's ordinary world.**

A crisis should be an event that stabs deeply into the hero. It is Frodo learning that the ring he possesses is sought by cruel wraiths who will murder him to obtain it. It is storm troopers destroying Luke Skywalker's farm, killing his aunt and uncle. It is a wardrobe leading to Narnia, Lucy's visit to the magical place, and the kidnapping of a faun she now must rescue.

Frodo had to leave the Shire, his beloved home. Luke no longer had a home, forcing him to join a mysterious mentor. Lucy had to leave her war-torn home and explore an enchanting, though dangerous new reality. Their ordinary worlds, that is, the lives to which they were accustomed, were gone, perhaps forever.

In *Reapers*, the crisis is the unexpected appearance of Alex and her arrest and prosecution of an innocent family, a family Phoenix dearly loved. He could no longer continue with his daily existence. He had to step out of his ordinary world and into a new and far more dangerous one.

Sometimes authors might employ multiple events to build a crisis. Then a "final straw" triggers the hero's response. Such a scenario is realistic, but it has a weakness. It doesn't allow the hero to reflect on a single horrific moment and wish it had never happened. In the single-event scenario, as the story unfolds, the benefits of the hero's actions come to light. He can reflect again and realize that the crisis was all for the best. A more trivial event that was merely the final straw lacks that power.

2. The crisis creates a goal, the objective of the story.

In the ordinary-world portion of the story, we established a goal for our hero, one that related to his normal way of life. Because of the crisis event, a new goal arises, an object of desire that is bigger in importance and in scope. It is a goal that forces the hero to look beyond his ordinary existence and perform in a way to which he is unaccustomed. He must leave his ordinary world, whether physically, spiritually, and/or emotionally, in order to achieve it.

This goal will become the driving force behind the hero's actions for the majority of the rest of the story. It will carry him through every conflict with the villain, seep into his motivations as he plans his next steps, and remind him of his purpose if he is tempted to go off course or even retreat.

As I mentioned earlier, in *Reapers*, Phoenix's new goal is to save an unjustly accused and condemned family from execution, and the goal is later further enhanced when he discovers more families who are facing the same fate. This is a driving force that grabs his mind like the jaws of a bulldog and refuses to let him go.

The establishment of an urgent goal is critical, because it must keep your readers engaged throughout the story. As you make sure the goal is always on the hero's mind, it will stay in readers' minds as well. Not only that, an urgent, must-have goal will motivate you as an author to finish writing the story. Readers will feel the intensity that you pour into the tale.

3. Achieving the desired goal is dangerous.

If the goal has no danger associated with it, then any sense of triumph or joy that comes from achieving it would be missing. How much satisfaction would you get from crossing a deserted, one-lane street on smooth pavement with healthy legs? You wouldn't even think about it, and you wouldn't tell the tale to others. It would be boring. No one would care to hear it.

But if you have to cross a busy Interstate highway, limping because of a bullet wound in your leg, while trucks zoom by, unable to see you because it's the middle of the night during a torrential downpour, and you finally get safely across, what is the sensation? Relief? Certainly. Joy? Probably. Would you tell the story to others? I would, and my friends and family would sit in rapt attention as I breathlessly provided the slippery, horn-blaring, dead-of-the-night details.

What is the difference between the two scenarios? Danger. Potential death or injury. These possible outcomes make readers pay attention. Worry about the hero is a huge attraction. We must include such danger throughout the story. The more, the better.

Yet, danger doesn't have to be physical. Sometimes the most compelling dangers are emotional, psychological, or relational. Will the hero's reputation get ruined? Might he forfeit the love or trust of his family members? Could he lose his sanity? All of these are realistic, and readers can relate to the perils.

In *Reapers*, Phoenix knows that one false step will mean his death, and he will face that possibility at every turn. Also, intense heartache arises when the villain stabs at his point of vulnerability. As the story progresses, multiple dangers, both physical and emotional, potentially lurk in every shadow.

4. Motivation to achieve the goal must be strong, both externally and internally.

In the ordinary world section, I discussed the need

for clarity of the hero's motivations in pursuing the initial goal. Readers want to understand why the hero is making his choices. Now that we have added danger to the new goal, this factor is even more important.

If a hero chooses to pursue the goal, and the dangers along the way are potentially deadly, causing a great amount of suffering no matter the outcome, then the motivations have to be equally great. In other words, the goal, in the hero's mind, must be worth the suffering necessary to accomplish it. Failing to match the motivations to the danger will result in readers not believing that the hero would endure the suffering.

Let's look at a simple example. Suppose a boy scout is on one side of a street, and a lost kitten is on the other. The scout crosses the street, picks up the kitten, reads the tag on the collar, and restores the kitten to its home.

Were you captured by this story? Did you feel worry for the scout or hope for the kitten's safety? I doubt it. There was too little danger.

So, we add danger. Traffic is heavy. Cars and trucks are zooming by, and there is no traffic light to stop them, even for a moment. Would the scout risk his life to cross the street to rescue the kitten? Some readers would doubt it. The kitten will probably eventually find its way home, or the owner would come and look for it. There is no sense in risking one's life for such a small gain. In fact, the scout might simply pull out his cell phone and call a friend who lives across the street. Let him rescue the kitten.

Because danger is now at a higher level than the motivations, we need to increase the motivations. Let's say that there is no time for someone else to rescue the kitten. The poor, shivering animal is in the clutches of a villain who is ready to scorch it with a flamethrower. Why? We don't know. We know only that the kitten is in immediate peril.

Our intrepid boy scout must act immediately. He will shout and wave his arms to stop traffic, thereby facing a modicum of danger, then cross at a gallop to foil the villain's dastardly plans.

Is this an interesting story yet? Not really. The goal is still lacking, motivation is weak, and the danger is still at a low level. Let's increase the obstacles another notch.

Instead of heavy traffic, artillery tanks are sitting on the street, poised with laser-guided shells to obliterate anyone who tries to cross. Now what will the scout do? The level of danger is astronomical, and readers might not believe that he would risk his life to save a kitten, no matter what the kitten's end might be.

To combat that possibility, we need to elevate the goal to match the danger. Let's say that this is a magic kitten, and its fur cures cancer. The scout knows this ability, and his motivation to save it increases greatly. What will he do? Maybe he will sniper crawl across the street, staying low so the tanks can't lock on him. Even if he fails to arrive in time to save the kitten, he has to try.

We have increased the value of the goal. That gives us an opportunity to match it with more danger. Let's add tarpits to the street and cobras lying in wait between the pits. If the scout tries to sniper crawl, he could either fall into a pit or be bitten by a cobra.

Yes, the story is ridiculous, but I am employing absurdity to illustrate a point. Although the intensity is much higher on both the goal side and the danger side, is the story compelling? Will readers believe that the scout will take the deadly risks? I think the answer is no to both questions. Why? Because to this point, the scout's motivations are external. His driving force has no internal components. Saving a kitten is honorable, to be sure, and he will receive praise for doing it, but we have provided no motivation that will make everyone believe in his willingness to suffer to such a great extent.

To provide a believable motivation, we need to look at the heart. We need to supply an internal component.

Let's say that the kitten's fur cures the scout's mother's cancer.

Now what will the scout do? He'll grab the closest cobras, tie them together into a lasso, and throw one end over a lamppost. Then he'll swing across the street, subdue the villain, and take the kitten to the laboratory where some of its fur will be humanely removed for the scout's dear mother and anyone else who needs it. Nothing will stop him, and readers will understand his death-defying obsession. It's all about love.

The internal motivation is the key. Frodo was willing to suffer all kinds of torture, not only because the forces of Mordor were evil, but also to save the Shire, his beloved home. Luke Skywalker also suffered, not only to stop the evil empire but because he wanted to become a Jedi Knight like his father. Lucy Pevensie was willing to face dangers aplenty, including the dreaded white witch, not just for the sake of a faun and talking beavers, but because the witch was ravaging a sparkling new world, much like Nazi bombs were ravaging her own home. And she also hoped to restore her wayward brother.

These are motivations of the heart, and nothing is more powerful than love.

To create the most compelling story possible, make the goal dangerous. Force the hero to endure immense suffering. But, most important, give him motivations of the heart that will make the suffering worthwhile. Then readers will relate to him, believe in him, and cheer him on from the beginning to the end, no matter what that end might be.

Take note that *Reapers* is a dystopian tale, which means that it starts out dark and is infused with oppression. The hero faces many failures that result in trouble, turmoil, and even death. Your story, on the other hand, might be lighter and include more success than failure.

As you consider inserting obstacles and the hero's motivations and sacrifices to overcome them, keep in mind your genre and your target audience. You might not want your story to be as dark as my dystopian examples.

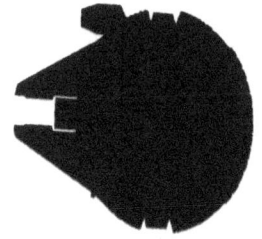

Pursuit of the Goal

Once the crisis event has concluded and the goal has been established, the hero will begin his pursuit of that objective. Since this section makes up the majority of your story, we will spend quite a bit of time describing it.

Following is a list of items to include in this story section.

- **Bring in forces of antagonism to block the hero's pursuit.**
- **Include rest periods after each conflict.**
- **Increase your hero's efforts with each attempt to achieve the goal, and increase your villain's counter-efforts, thereby creating escalating conflict.**

Let's look at each item in turn.

Conflict with The Villain

Bring in forces of antagonism to block the hero's pursuit.

If the hero is able to achieve the goal without any obstacles, our story would be a poor one indeed. We need an opposing force, a villain who tries to block our hero's efforts.

In literary terms, the hero is often called the protagonist, though the two words are not synonyms. The protagonist is always a story's key player. He often makes the decisions that drive the plot, and he usually undergoes the most internal changes. Yet, he is not always heroic in some story structures, such as redemption stories or tragedies. In the hero's journey structure, however, the protagonist is almost always the hero as well, which is why I equate the two for the purposes of this book.

Since the protagonist drives the story forward, we need an antagonist to try to block those efforts.

Forces of antagonism vary. They can be personal, that is, they can be villains who are motivated by self-interest or evil desires. They can be impersonal, such as forces of nature, disease, poverty, or government bureaucracy. Either type is realistic, and readers have likely faced both personal and impersonal antagonism themselves, making it easy for them to relate.

I prefer an antagonist with human-like responses, especially in fantasy or science fiction. Such a villain can react to the choices a hero makes and can devise a counter measure in direct response, thereby making the conflict personal. An impersonal force is unable to accomplish that feat.

Personal villains are also more complex. They have their own set of motivations, and these should be realistic and believable. As readers, we likely won't agree with a villain's motivations, but at least we should be able to understand them. A villain who acts out of insanity and therefore has no rational reasons for what he does is a weaker character, and it is a sign of lazier storytelling.

A well-developed villain should also be stronger than the hero in some ways, making it seem unlikely that the hero can defeat him. For example, at the beginning of the story, could a hobbit the size of Frodo defeat the great Sauron? Not likely at all. Could Luke Skywalker best Darth Vader, the metal-clad monster who could lift a man with one hand and throw him across a room? Certainly not. Could little Lucy Pevensie face the white witch who could turn anyone to stone with her wand? Preposterous.

The unlikeliness of victory is a compelling factor, and it enhances the joy of triumph when the hero actually defeats the more powerful villain.

Yet, take note that the villain's superiority need

not be in the category of physical strength. He can instead be much smarter, like a mad scientist who invents deadly weapons that can disintegrate the hero and his allies. The villain can be charming and charismatic, like a politician who gains the trust and alliance of everyone in power while our hero is vilified and ostracized. Impersonal antagonists should also seem insurmountable, such as a deadly disease without a cure, a famine that has wiped out thousands of farms, or a monstrous storm that is destroying everything in its path.

Now that we know how to set up a blocking force, let's go back to the hero's quest. When he strives to attain the story's goal, he will naturally seek to do so in what appears to be the easiest and most straightforward way. This plan, however, must be at cross purposes to what the villain wants. Frodo wanted to take the ring of power to Elrond to learn how to keep it out of the hands of Sauron. Sauron wanted to take the ring for himself, a direct contradiction. Therefore, while Frodo chose what appeared to be the simplest route to find Elrond, Sauron sent his ring wraiths to kill Frodo and steal the ring.

This meeting of opposite forces ignites a conflict, in this case a physical battle. Conflicts can be mental, emotional, or psychological, such as when a hero must do mental battle with the demons of his past.

In a conflict, the hero is blocked from achieving the story's goal, though he can make positive steps in that direction. If he were to achieve the goal after only one attempt, it would be too easy, and both the hero's and a reader's satisfaction would be minimal. Therefore, the hero should suffer, the frequency and level of suffering dependent on the darkness of your chosen genre.

Once the hero's attempt is blocked, he won't give up. He will seek another way to achieve the story's big goal, but before he does, the author needs to provide a rest period, which I will describe soon.

These three factors—the hero's attempt, the villain's blocking action that results in a conflict, and a rest period—create a cycle of conflict that will repeat through the rest of your story until the hero and villain meet in the ultimate conflict.

Each conflict in your cycles should have the following characteristics:

- The hero has a short-term goal that he hopes will pave the way for achieving the long-term goal.

- This smaller goal should be specific and clear. Readers should know what it is and how this step will aid the hero's effort to attain the long-term goal.

- The smaller goal should be something he thinks he can gain in a short amount of time. This way, readers believe they will see the outcome of this attempt quickly, which will keep them engaged.

- The goal should stay at the center of attention during the scene. Don't allow tangents to break the focus. Also, make this smaller goal urgent enough to keep readers' tension at a heightened level.

- Achieving this goal should not be easy. One or more obstacles should stand in the way, and the hero must respond to each obstacle.

For example, in *Reapers*, Phoenix's long-term goal is to rescue prisoners from the corrections camp. In order to do that, he has a short-term goal, to smuggle Singapore into the camp to help him.

In order to achieve this goal, he decides to sneak out of the camp undetected, but there is a prison guard at the exit, which is the first obstacle. In response, Phoenix employs a little ghost girl as a distraction.

> I grasped the door's lever and gently tried to push it down. Locked. Bending low, I whispered, "Okay, Tori, you disappear, stick your head through the door, and come back to tell me if you see a guard."
>
> Tori grinned. "This should be fun."
>
> Shanghai gave me the flashlight and backed away, whispering, "I'll go to my room. It'll be dark, Tori, so I'll look for your eyes when you come."
>
> As soon as Shanghai walked out of sight, Tori pushed her head through the door. After a few seconds, she drew it back in. "I saw a guard smoking a cigarette." She stuck out her tongue. "Yuck."
>
> "Okay. Now go visible. You know the plan."

Tori crouched in the corner. "I'm ready."

"Good." I turned off the flashlight, knocked on the door, and pressed my body against the corner opposite Tori's.

A husky voice penetrated the metal. "Who is it?"

I waited, saying nothing. Tori's eyes glowed more brightly, whether from delight or fear, I couldn't tell.

After a few seconds of silence, I reached from my hiding place and knocked again.

The guard called out, "Listen, no one's on the list for pre-authorized exits, so if it's an emergency, go to the main gate and report."

I waited a few more seconds, then knocked a third time and squeezed again into the corner. I imagined the guard looking through the window, his shifting eyes unable to catch sight of either of us.

"Some prankster in there is going to be in big trouble." Beeps sounded, then metal scraping on metal. The moment the door opened, Tori jumped up and ran outside.

"Hey!" A tall guard gave chase and faded quickly in the darkness.

> Just before the door swung closed, I slid through the gap and ran across a strip of grass, illuminated by the glow of two searchlights that swung toward the direction Tori had run. When I reached the street, I ducked behind a parked car. The guard stood near the side of the Hilton, scratching his head under his cap, the two searchlights locked on him.
>
> I rose slowly and backed away. So far, everything had worked perfectly.

Whether or not the hero succeeds with his response to the obstacle is up to you as the author. It's helpful to allow some successes and some failures so that readers won't be able to predict the outcome of any individual attempt.

In Phoenix's case, he had to take several steps to achieve this short-term goal. Most of them worked, and he was able to sneak Singapore into the camp, but some missteps caused a lot of grief later, which is a good mix of outcomes.

With some short-term goals, the villain might not be involved directly. His minions or other indirect forces in alliance with him can create the obstacles. Yet, we should show that the villain is informed about what the minions know, and he adjusts to the hero's actions accordingly.

In *Reapers*, the villain, Alex, suspects that Phoenix is trying to recruit Singapore. That prompts her to visit Singapore's apartment.

Sing rose, turned on her flashlight, and aimed the beam at Alex. "Are you a death messenger?" Sing called.

"No." Alex strolled into the alley, her hands in her jacket pockets as she angled her head upward. "My name is Alex, and I'm looking for Phoenix. I heard someone trying to get into your apartment building, but whoever it was left before I could get to the door. I thought it might be him."

Sing shone the light on the fire-escape ladder below. The spring-loaded hinges had brought it back to its horizontal perch well above the alley pavement. "Some guy tried to climb that ladder a few minutes ago. It makes quite a racket, so I came out here to see if a death messenger was trying to contact me. I scared him away, whoever he was, but he wasn't Phoenix. Too short and scrawny."

"When was the last time you saw Phoenix?"

Alex's appearance presented a new obstacle, which came about because of the villain's direct response to the hero's attempt to gain an advantage, and that obstacle increases the uncertainty of the hero's ability to achieve the goal.

Uncertainty is a powerful device. It makes readers worry along with the hero. We know that the villain is wise to the hero's attempts, but we're uncertain how much he knows and what he'll do with the knowledge.

In summary, use all of the following methods to your advantage:

- Short-term goals for the hero that will help with the long-term goal.

- Obstacles set up by the villain that block the short-term goals.

- Conflicts that are in multiple categories, whether physical, mental, or emotional.

- A mixture of successes and failures in achieving the short-term goals.

- Frequent uncertainty about the villain's knowledge and planned steps.

- Recycle the above until you come to the ultimate conflict.

Rest/Regain Strength

Include rest periods after each conflict.

After a conflict, which should include intensity that is physical, mental, and/or emotional, the hero needs an opportunity to rest. Rest, of course, is natural after a battle, and it serves purposes that go beyond simple restoration of muscles and mind.

During this period, the action slows down. The hero becomes contemplative. He reflects on successes, failures, and lessons learned. His actions become proactive instead of reactive, that is, he makes careful decisions based on experience gleaned from the past instead of instant decisions based on what is happening to him in the present.

Readers saw the hero in this state at the beginning of the story during the Ordinary World scene. The hero was in a proactive state, acting according to his experience and wisdom gained from his usual activities. He wasn't reacting to hurried, frenetic stimuli such as we see in conflict scenes.

This rest period, therefore, allows readers to

compare the hero's mental and emotional state after a conflict to his earlier state in the ordinary world. Has he changed? If so, in what way? Has he grown in wisdom? Are his rough edges getting smoother? Is he becoming more aware of his weaknesses and learning how to overcome them?

During a rest period, you have an opportunity to bring internal changes toward the surface, and these are usually associated with one or more themes in your story. If the hero is immature at the beginning, show him growing in maturity. If he lacks mercy, show the rudiments of mercy coming forth. If he needs to gain courage to face the problems in his world, show that courage beginning to rise.

This is not easy. You shouldn't show the changes coming about like an erupting volcano. They should simmer before heating to a boil, and the increases should manifest in a natural way. The obstacles he has faced, the allies he has consulted with, and the circumstances that helped him overcome obstacles to gain short-term goals should work together to help the hero understand the need to change and how to bring the change about.

The rest period should also be a time for the hero to plan his next action, and the changes he undergoes can be the impetus to persevere through a difficult challenge or maybe plot a new course instead.

For example, in *Reapers*, Phoenix successfully rescued the unjustly accused family from scheduled execution in the prison camp, but he discovered that many other innocent people were there who also needed to be rescued. During the rest period between the conflicts, he contemplates the world around him and its many troubles. His interior monologue explores his role in how to help solve the problems.

In the past, he has been content to just do his job and help in small ways where he can. He is a nobody who is unable to do more than that. Yet, the conflicts have shown him that this is not enough. He has to rise to another level and become the hero everyone needs. He has to embrace courage and realize that if he doesn't step up, maybe no one will. Now, as he rests, the idea that he must do more comes to the surface.

> While Sing and Shanghai curled on their cushions, I laid my head and shoulders on mine, my feet propped on the roof's parapet. A cool breeze wafted over the warm rooftop, caressing my cheeks with shifting temperatures that soothed my tired body. Sleep would come soon. I could feel it.
>
> A few stars shone through the haze, a rare sight in the city. Ever since the meltdown, no one in Chicago bothered to gaze at the heavens. The specter of what couldn't be seen ... or reached ... brought to earth the choking reality of our condition. We were trapped, human waste unable to escape from a tawdry shell, this dumpster called life.
>
> And I was a waste-disposal unit, destined to haul forsaken souls to a shadowy

door that opened to the unknown—the Gateway, that unexplained beyond-reproach expectation of release from this festering cavity.

A horn blared far away. A woman shouted, something about burning her hand on a candle, likely a cry of pain echoed within many a wall in the windy city. With electricity cut-off hour now past, the lights-out routine had been repeated a million times from row house to row house, from shanty to shanty. The jungle natives did what they could to survive.

In my mind, a thousand matches touched a thousand candlewicks, giving light to an equal number of darkened chambers. A man carried a silver taper to a bedroom and checked on three sleeping children crowded on a bed. The wavering light fell across the contented faces, giving the man reason to sigh with relief.

A woman probed a pantry with the light of a stubby red candle, hoping to find something to prepare for the next day's meals. Her hands trembling, she grasped a can of beans, then a bag of rice, a thin smile on her face—one more day her children could go to bed without the pangs of hunger.

> And in the glow of a flickering unity candle, two inches high and blackened by decades of anniversary celebrations, an old man kissed a frail old woman, slid into bed with her, and blew out the flame.
>
> The scene faded to gray, then to black. All was silent. The city waited anxiously for dawn. They waited for someone to rise up and prove that their hopes and prayers weren't for naught. They needed a courageous warrior who would open the gate and show them the other side of eternity.

Rest periods are also a good place to provide vivid descriptions and complex prose. The pace is slower, allowing for a slower reading pace. Also, your readers are emotionally hooked, and they will enjoy the details, the contemplation, and the dive into the character's soul.

This particular rest period also illustrates that the hero's long-term goal can change during the story. The crisis that drove Phoenix out of his ordinary world has been alleviated. He has achieved the goal that the crisis created. Now he knows that it's not enough. The real crisis has been hurting people for years. This family was merely a symptom of a deeper cancer. And now the long-term goal has changed. The conflicts must continue.

Greater Conflict

Increase your hero's efforts with each attempt to achieve the goal, and increase your villain's counter-efforts, thereby creating escalating conflict.

With each conflict, let the hero gain something that will help him succeed in achieving the story's long-term goal at a later time. This gained asset can be as simple as wisdom or experience. It can be a new magical power or a weapon. He can acquire a helpful ally or a document that provides information about the villain or a secret hideout. The options are boundless.

After a rest period, the hero will make another attempt to gain the long-term goal, and that attempt will be a more capable effort because of what he gained in previous conflicts.

This greater capability will prompt the villain to counter the hero with a stronger blocking force, thereby escalating the conflict. As the story continues through this cycle of attempts, blocking measures, conflicts, and rest periods, the conflicts will continue to escalate, which causes readers to anticipate an ultimate conflict in the future. And that is exactly what you will deliver at the proper time.

In *Reapers*, Alex learns about Phoenix's temporary disappearance from the prison and confronts him, thereby creating a new obstacle. She knows he's up to something, though she is unaware that Singapore is now in the corrections camp.

> When I arrived at the dining area, Alex stood at the doorway, dressed in her usual leather getup, a Styrofoam cup of coffee in her hand. Before I could get a look inside, she threw the cup into a trash can, grabbed my arm, and pushed me to the lobby. "That stunt you pulled last night nearly got two guards fired."
>
> "What do I care about your guards?" I jerked away and straightened my sleeve. "I already told you I'm trying to figure out a way to spring Colm's family, so I went exploring. You shouldn't act so surprised."
>
> "You think you're so smart." Alex lifted a hand as if to slap me but quickly lowered it. With her jacket open, the holster and gun came into view. "If a guard catches you out past curfew, the orders are to shoot to kill. Got it?"

"I'm in lockdown now. I couldn't leave my room at night if I wanted to."

She pushed my valve button, making it protrude. As energy leaked out, she grabbed a fistful of my hair and slammed my head against the wall. "Just remember our deal. You'll cooperate with the reapings. No complaints, or I'll make you shrivel." She let go of my hair and pressed my valve stem back in place. "Understood?"

Yet, Phoenix uses something that he gained earlier, microphones that Alex planted to spy on him. This allows him to overcome the new obstacle as the scene continues.

"I remember the deal." Ignoring a blossoming headache, I dug into my pocket and pulled out the microphones. I grasped her wrist and slapped them into her palm. "I'm not the one with the bad memory."

Alex clenched her fist around them. Lines dug into her brow, etching a menacing scowl. "It's going to be a pleasure watching your smart-aleck smirk wilt when the prisoners start dropping like flies. You have no idea what you're in for."

My throat tightened, but I resisted swallowing. "I'm a Reaper. I'll do my job."

The microphone revelation gives Phoenix an advantage, a position of confidence. He has thwarted Alex's surveillance and her physical threat by showing that he is on to her tricks. Still, Alex obviously has another plan in the works, something more sinister that will block Phoenix, and this raises another uncertainty and more tension. Readers know that Alex will find a way to neutralize Phoenix's recent gains, both his own boost of confidence and Singapore's presence, and readers will look forward to seeing how that comes about.

The Ultimate Conflict

This is the scene your readers have been waiting for. They have anticipated this climax with great eagerness. Don't let them down.

In order to prepare readers for the big battle, it's important to raise anticipation by keeping the heat rising during previous conflicts. This way, readers will be increasingly engrossed, and with the other conflicts proving to be so intense, they might not even realize which one is the biggest.

We want to avoid a common malady in many stories—the sag in the middle. After an exciting early conflict that features superheated action, stories often stagnate. They grow cold.

That's why we have to turn up the heat. Even during rest periods, the intensity should continue. The hero never loses sight of his goal. It is urgent. He has to get there no matter what.

We do raise the heat by continuing to apply methods we have already discussed.

1. **Include pre-conflict pauses.**
2. **Allow successes along with failures.**
3. **Create bigger obstacles to block the hero and force greater sacrifices.**

1. **Include pre-conflict pauses.**

One reason the middle portions of a story can feel cold is that readers might lose track of what's at stake. Realizing the consequences of potential failure is a must. Before some of the conflicts, perhaps all of them, add a pause to remind readers of the goal, the imminent danger, and what might be lost if the character fails. This will raise the heat and build intensity.

Here is such a pause in *Reapers*:

> When we arrived within the pedestals' triangle, I looked past the squirming figure in the chair and scanned the yard. Twilight had descended, making it difficult to see the prisoners' living quarters, especially with the searchlights nearly blinding us to everything beyond the makeshift arena.
>
> By now, Sing was probably inside the quarters, and with the spotlights already frozen on the center of the yard, she could make her escape move at any time. Since the guards had been doubled, she would have to overpower two guards twice—once at the door to the quarters and again at the Hilton's rear exit when

The Ultimate Conflict | 77

> they opened the door in response to her knock. With each passing moment, every step in our plan seemed more unlikely to work.
>
> Still, if anyone could do it, Sing could. I had to keep my hopes alive, though trying to free Cairo really complicated matters. Our chances of escape were as thin as the smoke in our capsules.

As you can see, there is no direct action in these three paragraphs. It is a pause. The hero is taking in the scene and contemplating the problems, the potential solutions, and what's at stake. It also shows that he is worried because the outlook is grim. This pause should reveal the hero's anxiety and infuse it into readers.

2. Allow successes along with failures.

If your hero always fails, then your reader will become frustrated, so allow some successes. Yet, don't allow success to remove the tension. Success in one goal should lead to a revelation of an even greater goal with higher stakes, as I have mentioned before.

And since you have blended failures with successes, readers won't be certain that the hero will prevail even in the ultimate climax scene. This uncertainty will heighten tension and keep the pages flipping.

Here is an example of a success and the revelation of a greater goal from *Reapers*:

> I gave Sing a quick summary of what happened while she was breaking the

family out of the camp, including our staged battle to the death and Alex's constant enticement to take the energy from the depot tube, though I left out the part about Kwame ... for the time being.

When I finished, I turned toward Sing. "So, where are the Fitzpatricks?"

"They're safe with my people," Sing said as she leaned her head against my shoulder. "The hardest part was relocking the door after I got them out. At least the prisoners I left behind were smart enough not to bang on it, but some of the women were crying. It broke my heart."

"I can imagine."

"And I have bad news. I heard Cairo's a prisoner in the camp now. I didn't see him or else I would've asked him to help me. He's in danger because Alex plans to terminate fifty prisoners each day until they're all dead and reaped."

"Fifty!" An image of Cairo playing his cello flashed to mind, then dozens of faces in the camp's living quarters. We had to get them all out, and we needed lots of help.

Phoenix and company succeeded in rescuing the family, but Alex, the antagonist, retaliates and threatens many more lives. Success was short-lived, and now Phoenix has a greater goal to achieve.

Any sag in the story's middle is thereby avoided. Goals increase. Conflict escalates. Tension mounts. And readers feel the heat.

3. Create bigger obstacles to block the hero and force greater sacrifices.

As the story continues, make the hero's obstacles bigger than the earlier ones. Your hero should be growing in wisdom and in heart, so he should be ready to tackle something tougher. Yet, each obstacle should seem even greater than what your character can handle.

These increases in difficulty, as well as the conflict necessary to overcome new obstacles, keep readers enthralled. How is the hero going to manage this new blockade? Will he fail like he did with some other obstacles?

As you make the obstacles bigger, raise the stakes as well. The consequences of failure become horrific, and the benefits of success are heightened. The battles are more intense, and the suffering worsens. The hero must fight harder every step of the way.

Challenge the hero to make greater and greater sacrifices, including those that cause emotional torture. Here are some ways to accomplish this.

- **Impossible Dilemmas**
- **Double Jeopardy**
- **The Black Moment**
- **The Point of No Return**
- **All Factors Culminate at Once**

Impossible Dilemmas: An impossible dilemma occurs when the hero is faced with two or more options. Each option is crucial, and choosing any option will cause great harm if the other options are not accomplished. To the hero and the readers, it seems impossible to choose more than one.

Force the hero to choose between two high priorities, perhaps a love from the past, whether romantic or otherwise, and a love that blossomed during the story, and losing either of them would shred the hero's soul.

Before the ultimate conflict's dilemma, you need to prepare readers by providing other dilemmas that get worse with each choice, thereby turning the heat up in measured doses.

In speculative fiction, the antagonist sometimes intentionally sets up a dilemma in order to break the hero's resolve. If one of his loves is destroyed, then he will despair or doubt himself, making him more vulnerable to future attacks.

The antagonist might also use the choice to lure a new ally. In theory, the hero will choose against someone, and that person will then be open to the antagonist's lure. "You see, the hero doesn't really love you. He would have let you die, but I saved you. That proves that I have been telling you the truth all along."

An impossible dilemma forces the hero to dig deep into his soul and decide which option is more important to him. It will reveal his strengths and expose his weaknesses. It can also show his ingenuity as he tries to come up with a way to foil the dilemma by finding a way to solve the dilemma and bring about the desired results for both choices.

Sometimes the hero solves the dilemma and foils the antagonist's plans. Maybe he tries to choose both options and he fails to secure either victory, thereby suffering a double loss. Sometimes he chooses one option over the other and has to face the consequences, and the author can decide how to bring those about.

Maybe the consequences of his choice are tragic, adding to the sufferings inherent in a difficult journey. Maybe the blow is softened because the hero's character qualities are admired by another powerful force in the story. Maybe the person he chose to save will become an amazing new ally who can do something to reverse the effects of the tragedy of the choice not taken. These author decisions are many and varied.

With regard to turning up the heat, the dilemma itself is what matters. Make the dilemma truly gut-wrenching for the hero, something that will be worse than any nightmare, and make it seem that there is no way out.

Often great dilemmas are not intentionally invented by the antagonist. Pay the kidnapper's ransom, or call the police? Negotiate with the terrorists, or attack their hideout? Go away to school and pursue a career, or stay home and take care of an ailing mother, perhaps for years? These down-to-earth dilemmas happen all the time, so put your hero square in the midst of such heart-rending choices. Make the character sweat, squirm, and weep over the options, and your readers will commiserate on a deep emotional level.

In *Reapers,* I created a dilemma by attacking Phoenix's vulnerability point, Misty. As I mentioned before, I foreshadowed this vulnerability early in the story and reminded readers of it from time to time in order to keep the thought fresh. Later, I introduced Shanghai, a new person for Phoenix to care for, thereby setting her up to become the other choice in the dilemma.

> Alex set the sonic gun at the back of Misty's head. "Feel free to converse, but don't take another step closer."
>
> "Misty!" I extended my arms, but they were way too short. "Are you hurt?"
>
> A sob contorted her face. Tears flowed. As she shook, her lips formed the first part of my real name, but she sucked it back and cried out, "Phoenix! Oh, Phoenix, I missed you so much!"
>
> "I missed you, too!" I tightened a fist and shook it at Alex. "Let her go! She's innocent! She hasn't done anything to deserve—"
>
> "Oh, shut up, Phoenix. I know that." Alex pressed the barrel against Misty's head, bending her neck forward. "This is unveiled, unbridled brute force. If I can get you to kill Shanghai, you'll be

mine forever, but I doubt that you yet know yourself the way I know you. You hand over slavish chains in a way you don't yet comprehend."

She nodded at the line of guards. "Four of you hold him. Don't underestimate his strength." Peter and three guards stalked toward me. I readied my fists and leaped at Alex. Peter grabbed my arm and jerked me backwards into the foursome's clutches. As I struggled to get free, he twisted my elbow with incredible strength. Pain rocketed to my brain, sending blinding flashes across my eyes.

"Stop it," Peter growled, "or I'll break your arm."

I swallowed through my dry throat. How could I save Misty when I couldn't even budge?

"Now, Phoenix ..." Alex's smile thinned out. "Who will live and who will die?"

The concept is straightforward. If the hero chooses one option, he gains something valuable while losing something valuable. He stops a tragedy and suffers a different one. Of course, choosing the other option does the same but with a swapping of consequences. The choices are both beneficial and terrible. And that dilemma turns up the heat, thereby keeping readers engrossed.

Double Jeopardy: A double jeopardy occurs when the hero faces more than one potential disaster at the same time.

For example, while the hero is trying to escape from a burning forest, a venomous snake bites him. Now he is threatened by fire and venom at the same time--a double jeopardy.

Since the hero has to solve two threatening problems instead of one, intensity is doubled. Even if he escapes the fire, how will he get to the hospital in time? If he stops to administer aid to himself, how will he protect himself from the fire?

A double jeopardy can also be constructed as an impossible dilemma. In the fire/venom scenario, the hero might think he has to choose between escaping the fire and stopping to try to administer a cure, and he sees no way to do both. Yet, such a dilemma isn't necessary for a simple double jeopardy situation. Two dangers at the same time are all that is needed to ramp up the excitement. Adding an impossible dilemma can inject even more intensity. It's up to you.

Examples:

Markus has to take the secret plans, handwritten on parchment, to the wizard, but he comes upon a river too wide and swift to swim across (jeopardy #1). While he is pondering what to do, rain begins to fall. He stuffs the parchment under his shirt, but the wetness bleeds through, smudging the ink (jeopardy #2).

Captain Zolt speeds the spaceship away from intergalactic bandits (jeopardy #1), but the refuge planet ahead explodes, sending debris zipping toward his craft (jeopardy #2).

Priscilla stands in the soup line with a bowl, her second time through. If Mistress catches her, she'll be whipped (jeopardy #1). She is getting soup for Mason, her sick brother who is hiding in the cellar in the girls-only home. No one knows he is still alive after his escape from prison. As she keeps her head low, two soldiers walk through the entry gate. One points at her and shouts, "There is Mason's accomplice. Arrest her." (jeopardy #2).

The ways to inflict a double jeopardy on your character are limited only by your imagination.

The Black Moment: A variation of the impossible dilemma. The hero believes that the dilemma is truly impossible. All is lost. He thinks he cannot achieve the story's long-term goal. His life's mission is being cast into a pit of darkness.

This is the moment that the character reaches deep inside and accesses new strengths he has gained or lessons he has learned during the journey to this point. These give him the ability to go on. Earlier, he could not have done this, so his suffering and trials are proven to have a purpose. As he realizes this, he gains even more strength, perhaps perceiving that a higher power is guiding his steps. He can go on. He must go on.

With this newly gained fortitude, he brushes himself off and marches confidently toward the story's ultimate conflict. He will need that bravado, because the worst is yet to come.

Such moments allow readers to commiserate with the character. Yes, he has suffered greatly and is rightfully near despair. Yet, readers also urge him to drag himself out of the pit. "You can do it! Remember what's at stake!" Then when he does, readers cheer for him all the more.

The Point of No Return: Something happens that cannot be undone.

Often, a point of no return occurs without a character's input, that is, the character has no power over it, such as a crisis that starts the hero's journey, or other factors outside of the character's control—a murder, a financial collapse, or a crippling disease.

The most intriguing points of no return occur when a character makes a decision that causes it, knowing that the decision cannot be reversed.

Readers are especially engrossed when the character realizes that the choice he makes will cause himself permanent harm but he decides to go ahead anyway, believing that his choice is for the greater good. In other words, he sacrifices to his own harm expecting that the harm can never be repaired. This is real love, and readers are captivated by it.

A good story has several of these points. Some are simple without high stakes, especially in the beginning stages. With each point of no return, the stakes can get higher and higher.

Here is an example from *Reapers*:

"Familiar?" Anger flickered in her eyes. "I attended reapings before you were born, and I have followed your career ever since—" Her brow furrowing, she picked up a pill from the mattress. "What is this?"

"Candy," I said without hesitating. "I always bring some when a dying child has siblings. Molly has two sisters."

"Is that so?" She extended her hand, her voice calm, even in the midst of Molly's continuing gasps for breath. "May I see your supply?"

I rose and patted my cloak, trying to ignore Molly's travail and her family's looks of desperation. "I gave them all away."

"You are kind to give so much to the grieving siblings." She sniffed the pill, then wrinkled her nose. "Or perhaps not so kind." Pinching the pill at arm's length, she scanned the room again, her eyes shifting from the night table to Molly to the family trio as they stood stock-still. Finally, she nodded at Colm and spoke with tightened lips. "Empty your pockets onto the bed."

After a quick glance at me, Colm dug into his pocket, pulled out the pill bottle, and dropped it to the mattress.

> Alex picked up the bottle. "An odd candy container, don't you think?" Her tone carried only the slightest hint of sarcasm.
>
> I focused on her gun, still visible inside her open jacket, likely a sonic gun—short-ranged, but deadly. Trying to disarm her meant I would have to kill her if I succeeded, or face execution if I failed. There had to be another way. "The pill bottle is mine. I traded for it at the shroud. I hoped to help Molly."

Phoenix knows that his admission will cost him something, and there is no turning back. Alex will know he is guilty. The cat is out of the bag. This is a point of no return.

As you escalate the stakes in these points of no return, readers look forward to an expected peak, and you can bring in the biggest point of no return when you introduce the story's culminating black moment.

A great example of a black-moment point of no return is in the movie *Tangled* when Flynn cuts Rapunzel's hair, a decision that he believes will bring about his own death. Yet, he carries it out anyway because the sacrificial act will set Rapunzel free by ensuring that her hair cannot be used to imprison her any longer.

The key elements of a point of no return include a dilemma and a decision that cannot be revoked, and the decision causes the hero to sacrifice for someone other than himself.

The Ultimate Conflict

All Factors Culminate at Once

Since you have used the first four elements in the list to turn up the heat, now you are ready for a climactic event—the ultimate conflict. For the climax, set up the most painful impossible dilemma yet, create a double jeopardy, plunge the character into a black moment, and force him to make a point-of-no-return decision.

For the ultimate conflict, if you haven't already done so, reach into the hero's past and attack the vulnerability point that you foreshadowed in the opening scene. Readers learned about the heart-wrenching issue long before it became part of a dilemma, such as Phoenix's love for Misty, first raised while Phoenix was looking at a photo of her.

At that point, the issue was inactive, that is, nothing about Misty was happening at the moment. Readers learned that Phoenix's heart was attached to her. That setup allowed the story to later stab the hero's soft spot. He had to choose between her and something else that grew in importance during the tale.

Since I forced that choice in an earlier impossible dilemma, I couldn't do it again in the ultimate conflict. I hoped to lead readers to believe that the earlier dilemma was the actual climax when, in fact, I was setting up the real climax by showing readers that failure was possible, which should make them worry that failure was also possible in the next apparent climax. The hero might actually fail to achieve the long-term goal.

For your climax setup, in the dilemma that precedes your ultimate conflict, if the hero succeeded in solving the dilemma, he needs a new goal that surpasses the one achieved by the success. A rest period following the previous dilemma is a good time for the hero to realize the necessity of the new goal. This creates the motivation to surmount the next obstacle, which will be the greatest one of all.

If the earlier dilemma results in failure for the hero, the choice the character makes can bring about some sort of success for someone, even if the hero loses something valuable in the process. Every dilemma choice needs a potential harm and a potential benefit. That benefit can come to the hero's aid during the next dilemma.

In the ultimate-conflict peak, the hero has a new choice to make in which the negative consequences of either option are worse than the consequences of the choices in the earlier dilemma. In other words, ramp up the tension even higher than you did before in a way that readers likely thought was impossible. Also, show how the hero is suffering both physically and mentally while desperately trying to solve this new impossible dilemma. The more the character suffers, the better the climax.

Following is the ultimate conflict from *Reapers*. Now Phoenix has to choose between killing his new friend, Singapore, or allowing Alex to kill innocent prisoners. If the prisoners die, he won't be able to achieve the long-term goal. If Sing dies at his own hand, he will suffer a horrific tragedy, the death of a friend who helped him get this far in the struggle.

> Alex stabbed a finger at Sing. "Kill her, Phoenix! Be done with this wanton wench. My guard at the prisoners'

residence building deceived you. Theresa deceived you. You are obviously too easily led by the nose. And now letting Sing live will serve only to prove your starry-eyed naïveté once again, and your unprecedented gullibility will mean the deaths of many children who just want a chance to leave this hellhole and go home in peace!"

Sing cried out, her words punctuated by gurgling gasps. "Do what ... you think is right ... I asked you to ... to trust me ... but either way you decide ... I'll still love you. ... I will always love you."

"More lies!" Alex shouted. "She has proven you can't believe a word she says. Kill her now and be done with it."

My entire body quaked. "I ... I can't."

Alex waved a hand at the prisoners. Theresa walked behind a woman and shot her with the sonic gun. The telltale pop jolted my brain. She twitched on the ground for a moment, then lay motionless. Like a vulture, Peter descended on her body and covered her with his cloak.

A little girl screamed, "Mommy!" Two men leaped to their feet, but when a guard grabbed the girl and set a gun to her head, the men dropped to their knees again.

My arm shook harder. I could barely keep the gun in place. A barrage of images blazed in my mind—Sing and Kwame and Alex and Shanghai—all spinning in a wild vortex. Finally, Mex's image blended into the turmoil. With desperate pulls, he struggled to free himself from the life-sucking vacuum, the death penalty so callously executed by the will of one of the Council's minions, a sentence delivered because of evidence planted on him, planted by a son and his mother who had conspired to bring about this end at this moment. If I killed Sing, they would have their victory. If I killed Sing, Alex would win. If I killed Sing, my heart would shrivel up and die.

"You've run out of time, Phoenix." Alex's tone was cold and cruel. "Kill her now, or a child is next. You know I won't hesitate."

Here are a few more points to consider as you plan your ultimate conflict scene.

Show the Goal Ahead of Time.

Readers need to know in specific and concrete terms what the hero is trying to achieve. It should not be nebulous, though it might seem unattainable.

For example, the goal should not be "Peace on Earth" or "Enough Food for Everyone." These are wonderful ideals, but they are not specific. They are pie-in-the-sky dreams. A more specific option for the peace ideal would be for the hero to stop an impending war between two kings by spoiling an assassination attempt. For the feeding-the-hungry hopes, maybe the hero could learn that a villain has pinched a supply line and is hoarding the supplies and selling them on the black market. The hero's goal, then, is to battle the forces that are redirecting the supplies and bring the villain to justice.

When readers are aware of exactly what the final goal is, the ultimate conflict is enhanced. They know what success and failure look like. They realize what's at stake.

Foreshadow the Final Conflict.

It helps readers to know what the conflict will look like. This makes anticipation grow. In the original Star Wars film, the leaders showed an animated hologram describing the planned attack on the Death Star and the goal of shooting a photon torpedo into a vent shaft. This allowed viewers to know what to watch for.

In the Lord of the Rings films, the story showed Elrond shouting at Isildur to throw the ring of power into Mount Doom, which directly foreshadowed Frodo's later attempt to do so.

With such foreshadowing, readers can imagine the hero making the attempt. This elevates anticipation and incites worry for the hero's sake.

Keep the goal in readers' minds.

The long-term goal should never be an afterthought. It should always be in the forefront of the hero's mind. The urgency should never waver. In fact, it should heighten as any delay in achieving the goal makes matters worse.

Have a face-to-face meeting before the final conflict.

Sometimes it's a good idea to show the hero and the villain meeting face to face before the ultimate conflict occurs. Readers will wonder if this will ignite a conflict at that moment, and tension will rise. But the two will have to stand down for the time being, maybe by their own choice or because of unavoidable circumstances.

For example, in *Star Wars*, Luke Skywalker sees Darth Vader kill Obiwan Kenobi. Then Vader turns to see Luke trying to escape with his allies. At that moment, the hero and the villain could do battle, and they probably would welcome the conflict, but a door closes between them, preventing the fight.

In the film *The Patriot*, the hero, Benjamin Martin, meets the villain, Colonel Tavington, nearly nose to nose. Tavington tries to goad Martin into a fight by telling him how much he enjoyed killing Martin's son, but Martin refuses to take the bait and promises to kill Tavington before the war is over.

The face-to-face meeting is intense and riveting, and viewers know that the real battle will eventually take place. In fact, because of this meeting and Martin's promise, they are begging for it to happen.

This face-to-face meeting is not essential. It is merely another intensity-building tool you might be able to use to your advantage.

Actual conflict – Exciting, intense, and the hero's defeat or death is possible.

The ultimate conflict scene needs to be the most intense of all. It should make some readers gasp, shake, or even cry. All hope should be lost, at least so it seems. Maybe every one of the hero's allies appears to have abandoned him, and he is alone against insurmountable odds. Because you have shown readers that the hero can fail at critical steps of the journey, maybe he will fail here as well.

In *Star Wars*, Luke is the only X-wing fighter left trying to destroy the Death Star. All other allied ships have been crippled or destroyed. His friend Han Solo left with his reward money, apparently satisfied with financial gain. The dreaded Darth Vader is chasing Luke and gets a computer target lock on him. Earlier, viewers saw that every similar lock resulted in the targeted ship getting destroyed. How could Luke escape? It seems impossible.

Take note, if important characters have died along the way, you have shown your readers that death is a distinct possibility. If you imply that the hero's death could bring about the long-term goal, then readers might wonder if the character will sacrifice himself to achieve it. Keep readers wondering, and the intensity will skyrocket.

Enemy vanquished?

The villain has opposed the hero since the beginning of the journey. If he has been cruel and murderous, readers will likely want to see him die, either directly by the hand of the hero or by the villain's own devices. Another option is to allow the people the villain has oppressed to rise up and do him in.

You could also let him live and suffer the humiliation of defeat. This would make readers wonder if he will regain power and attack the hero again, which, if you are planning a sequel, might be a great idea.

Beware, however. In a sequel, do not let the villain overcome the hero in ways he has in the past. The hero is stronger, wiser, and more experienced now. Any resurgence by the villain must come in more powerful or cunning ways. We don't want the hero to appear to be anything but a victorious warrior who doesn't slide back to foolish ways. He goes only forward to the next adventure.

Achieving the Goal: Resolution, Reward, and The New Ordinary World

Now that you have ramped up your story's intensity and brought it to a heart-racing climax, how do you finish? With peace and satisfaction. The action will drop to a lower level, to be sure, but that's fine. Your readers are ready for a well-earned rest.

First, let's look at the achieving of the story's overarching goal. After the ultimate conflict, it is essential for the hero to attain a critical goal. Readers have been cheering for him to do so since a goal was first revealed after the crisis that launched his journey.

Yet, the goal the hero started with might not be the one he envisioned at the beginning of the journey. The conflicts and suffering caused growth in experience, wisdom, and maturity. His view of the world could have changed, and his goal might have altered somewhat or shifted greatly.

For example, in the film *Ben-Hur*, Judah Ben-Hur was unjustly condemned to the galley ships, and his mother and sister were sentenced to the dungeon. Judah's goal, the objective that kept him struggling to survive, was to return to Judea and exact revenge upon Messala, the man who deceitfully arranged the punishment.

When Judah gets his revenge, he realizes that it's not satisfying. In fact, it made him feel emptier than ever. Later, when he meets Jesus Christ and learns about mercy and forgiveness, only then does he gain the real goal that his heart longed for. Only then could he rest from his years of conflict and suffering.

If you decide to shift the goal, be sure to foreshadow the shift. Don't spring it on your readers out of the blue. Show that the hero has been exposed to the idea of a different goal and that his need for it is growing and becoming more apparent.

In *Ben-Hur*, Jesus gives Judah water, helping him survive the torturous journey to the galley ships, and that gift plants the first seed of love and mercy. Then Judah meets one of the Magi who tells him that the lust for revenge he harbors within is wrong, that he must accept God's judgment. These seeds grow in Judah during the rest of the film.

In *Reapers*, Phoenix's overarching goal changed along the way. At first, he wanted to save a family. When he realized that many other families needed the same rescue, the goal shifted to a larger-scale goal. Singapore had been telling him about a greater need, and the death of his friend Mex provided more evidence, and doubts grew in Phoenix's heart. Later, when he saw the condemned families for himself, he realized that saving one family wasn't enough. A new goal manifested, and that drove his motivations through the rest of the story.

Whether you decide to keep the same goal throughout the story or not, it's crucial that the hero reaches a goal that is satisfying, one that helps others, the product of the hero's self-sacrificial acts.

After the hero achieves the goal, it's time to resolve the story. Writing teachers often call this stage the dénouement (pronounced day-noo-mah). The author resolves the conflicts, ties up the loose ends, and shows how the hero's world is better in some way than it was at the beginning of the story.

We started in the hero's ordinary world, and now we create a new ordinary world in which the character can rest and reflect. He usually realizes the importance of the themes we have included in the story, and he expresses sorrow over what he lost and joy over what he accomplished and gained.

In this section, we can show who survived, who died, who married, and who will go on with the hero in a sequel. Hero's journey stories often end with an awards ceremony, a royal coronation, a wedding, a funeral, or with a scene of departure for a new journey.

Let the characters' emotions flow. Let the hero say thank you to other characters without whom he could never have survived, good-bye to warriors who will now go in another direction, and hello to those who have been missing or are returning to the hero's life.

Yet, with all of this, we should make the scene short. Wrap it up and finish with a satisfying sigh of contentment. Readers usually prefer a wrap-up that doesn't linger too long. The exception is when we are writing the final book in a series. Readers who have come this far on a long, multi-volume journey will enjoy a more complete dénouement. They have learned to love the characters and want to know what happens to them in the long term.

Here are some elements to remember when writing the final scene:

- Readers need an emotionally satisfying ending. Satisfaction comes with a feeling of triumph, which comes from a victory against seemingly impossible odds.

- There must be some victory. If the story is a series, the first book might not have a complete victory, but at least a sense of accomplishment must occur.

- A scene after a victory often displays both agony and ecstasy. Victory that comes at great cost usually generates more emotion in a reader than if nothing was lost.

- The hero's courage and sacrifice are recognized and rewarded in some way. Readers want others to witness what they have witnessed, that this hero is really amazing.

- If victory wasn't complete, create the setup for a sequel. Show that the hero has another step to accomplish, though he is resting at the moment.

In many stories, the hero has to break away from the crowd and act alone, which makes his or her sacrifice, suffering, and courage all the more compelling, and that, in turn, magnifies the reader's emotional need to properly reward the character.

Unfortunately, when the hero takes the lonely road to achieve the goal, it is possible, even probable, that no one will know what the hero did to save everyone. And it seems self-serving for the hero to come home and blow his own horn about his achievements.

This is why authors need to make sure someone significant in the story, especially a character with higher standing than the hero, recognizes the hero's courage and sacrifice in a direct manner.

For example, I reviewed an early draft of *Precisely Terminated*. In this story, the heroine, Monica, endures incredible suffering and employs tremendous courage to save the lives of millions of people. Yet, because she did it alone, at the end of the story, only one other person knew what she did, and no one thanked her.

Because of this lack of recognition, as a reader, I felt empty and unfulfilled. I told Amanda she needed to add at least a word of thanks from someone who mattered to Monica. So Amanda went back to work and came up with this:

> She looked again at Simon. With his hands stuffed in his pockets, he gazed back at her, tears trickling from both eyes. Exhaling heavily, he shook his head sadly. "I'm sorry."

"Sorry?" Her voice rose barely above a whisper. "For what?"

He shuffled across the bridge, knelt in front of her, and looked into her eyes. "For everything. I have mistreated you, manipulated you, and ordered you around like my own slave. I should be shouting your praises from the rooftops." He took one of her bandaged hands and kissed her fingertips. "You, my dear, are a heroine, the savior of all Cillineese. You have given us hope. We see now that the Nobles' hold is vulnerable. You have loosened its grip of terror. Now all we need to do is find a way to strip their fingers away from our necks for good."

When I read this, I pumped a fist and whispered, "Yes!"

This kind of recognition channels a reader's emotions into the story. Readers know instinctively that good deeds should be rewarded, and when one significant character delivers that reward, even through simple verbal recognition, readers feel that their own desire to thank the hero has been fulfilled.

This need is beautifully illustrated in the film *Return of the King*. The four hobbits endured horrific suffering and achieved world-saving goals, but until the coronation scene near the end, their sacrifices had not been properly recognized. When the hobbits bowed to Aragorn, the new king, he said that they bow to no one. Then he and everyone else bowed to the hobbits.

How many viewers pumped a fist and whispered, "Yes!" when they saw this scene? I was among them.

It is true that real heroes sometimes don't receive the recognition they deserve, and you might want to write about a lonely hero who suffers and sacrifices without reward. Such a story can be compelling, and the lack of hero recognition can provoke strong emotions in readers. Yet, I urge authors to reward the character in some way. Public recognition might be inappropriate, but at least show that the hero has gained recognition and reward from someone, maybe a child or a peasant, or maybe from heaven through a beam of light from above.

In *Reapers*, Shanghai, a fellow Reaper whom Phoenix highly respects, recognizes his accomplishments in this way:

> Shanghai gripped my arm. "You didn't fail, Phoenix. You're the bravest person I've ever met. For three years you've risked your life to help the desperate people of this city, and you sacrificed everything you love to save those innocent prisoners. In my book, you're a hero."

Phoenix rescued the families in the corrections camp. He achieved the desired goal. Yet, that achievement helps him understand that there is still more to do. He needs to strike at the heart of the system that would imprison innocent people. He has to go to the

Gateway and learn the truth, which sets up the sequel and the next adventure.

Remember the negative emotions I listed earlier? Whichever emotions you selected to put into your opening scene, now is the time to resolve at least some of them with their corresponding positive emotions.

- Loss - Gain
- Sadness - Happiness
- Loneliness - Companionship
- Suffering - Healing
- Injustice - Justice
- Heartbreak - Restoration
- Betrayal - Trust
- Dissatisfaction - Contentment
- Withdrawal/Numbness - Renewal

You don't have to show that every negative emotion has been vanquished. In fact, that would be unrealistic, but it's a good idea to show that the hero has come to a new ordinary world that is a place to rest and find peace, at least for a while.

Sometimes the new ordinary world can feel bittersweet where pain and sadness blend with a muted victory. For example, in *Empire of the Sun*, the hero is a pre-teen boy named Jamie who gets separated from his parents while in China at the beginning of World War II. He surrenders to the Japanese and is put into a prison camp where he suffers greatly.

Jamie's goal, of course, is to survive the camp and find his parents. During his periods of suffering, he chooses to sacrifice for others to help them survive.

Although he started the tale as a spoiled rich kid, he transforms into a selfless servant.

At the end of the story, he is finally reunited with his parents, but he is broken and empty, having lost his childhood. As he hugs his mother, we see that this suffering hero can finally rest, though he has lost so much. It is truly bittersweet.

The simplicity of the Hero's Journey story structure allows for seemingly infinite possibilities at every story juncture. Along with endings that range from joyful to bittersweet, you can have multiple heroes and villains, side plots and minor characters, and multi-faceted goals that can be rejected and later restored. The only limit is the extent of your imagination.

Yet, the most important factor is bringing your readers with you on the journey. Part two of this book will provide some tools that will draw readers into your story and keep them there.

Write Them In Toolbox

Point of View

Motivation/Reaction Units

Narrative

Dialogue Mechanics

Interior Monologue

Show, Don't Tell

Foreshadowing

Tool #1 - Point of View

Point of view (POV) is how you show your story to readers. What perspective do you provide? Do you tell the story as if you are an all-knowing narrator (omniscient POV)? Do you tell the story from the perspective of one or more characters (third person POV)? Do you allow the character to tell the story (first person POV)?

In order to illustrate the differences, let's say that you are at a zoo. A guide takes you from exhibit to exhibit and describes the characteristics of each animal. The guide tells you about the animals' habits, native environment, and facts about the species that even the animals don't know. Your experience would be similar to reading a story written from an omniscient POV.

Now let's say that the guide strapped a mind-reading camera helmet on a gorilla and recorded everything the gorilla said, heard, and thought over the years. When you come to the zoo, the guide describes the sights, sounds, and thoughts that the recording device replays and nothing else. If the camera didn't record it, then the guide doesn't report it. The guide provides no commentary based on his own perspective. For you, this experience would be similar to reading a third-person-limited POV story.

Suppose you are sitting in an amphitheater at the zoo, and the gorilla himself walks onto the stage. He tells you his story himself, including his own commentary and reflections. This would be similar to reading a first-person POV story, that is, if you can get over the shock of hearing a talking gorilla.

Omniscient Point of View

Omniscient point of view is sometimes called the "narrator" point of view. When writing a scene in this perspective, you are an all-knowing narrator who is able to tell readers about any aspect of the story, the back story, or what will happen in the future. The perspective doesn't depend on any character's input, that is, even if the characters are not aware of something, you can still tell the readers about it.

For example, "Julie went to bed and slept peacefully, unaware that Tom would call in the morning to invite her to the park for a rousing round of hopscotch. If she had known that, she would likely have dreaded the call and tossed and turned all night."

This POV has some advantages. It's a good choice for a story that covers a long period of time. You can offer a panoramic sweep of scenes and events that are not narrowed to a particular character's perspective.

For example, you can tell a story about several generations in a family. In so doing, you can remind readers of past incidents characters might not know about. You can even mention that a current event will have significant future ramifications.

When writing omniscient POV, you should use third-person pronouns (he, she, it, they, them) for all characters. For example: "He drove Carla to the park where they met Tom and Julie and played hopscotch with the park's rangers."

Since you are the omniscient writer, you can dive into any character's mind and describe what he or she is thinking at any time. For example: "When Tom threw the beanbag to the third square, he wondered if the number three provided a sign. Perhaps he and Julie should get married in three days. That being the case, he would have to propose quite soon. She hated to be rushed."

In omniscient POV, unlike in other perspectives, you are allowed to describe the thoughts of multiple characters in the same scene, but you should avoid what we call "head hopping," that is, shifting from one person's thoughts to another's to another's. A quick succession of shifts can cause confusion in readers, which is, of course, undesirable.

In addition, with omniscient POV you have the freedom to provide commentary. For example, "So Tom died at the hands of Julie only hours before she committed suicide by swallowing a hopscotch beanbag. Tragedy is often the end of relationships that are based on foolish assumptions, conceived by shallow characters, and held together by hopscotch games in the park."

I advise, however, to avoid doing this. Although we see such commentary in some classic novels, most modern readers don't care for author intrusions. They want to know what the characters think and feel, not the author's opinions. Yet, a skilled author can still provide commentary in thematic ways without directly intruding.

A major disadvantage of omniscient POV is the distancing of readers from the scene. Modern readers enjoy feeling "inside" the story, being within the skin of a character, and experiencing an adventure through a character's perspective. Omniscient POV tends to give a helicopter feel to readers, as if they are hovering over the action instead of walking in the middle of it as one of the characters.

If you desire to communicate intimate closeness, then you should choose third-person-limited POV or first-person POV.

Third-person-limited Point of View

Third-person-limited is similar to omniscient in that the writer employs third-person pronouns (he, she, it, they, them) for all characters, including the POV character, that is, the scene's focal character. It is called "limited" because the writer describes only what the focal character sees, hears, smells, touches, or knows about.

For example, from my series Tales of Starlight, the following is the beginning of a scene written using this type of POV with Adrian as the focal character.

> Adrian dropped to his knees and laid Marcelle on the ground. As he panted,

cold air swirled, and light drizzle added wetness to his sweat-drenched tunic. Wallace and Shellinda, their sleeves now covering their arms, plopped down beside him. Both tilted their heads upward and opened their mouths to catch the tiny drops and quench their thirsts.

"Take your time and get as much as you can," Adrian said. "We'll rest here awhile."

Wallace laid the sword on the ground. "Want me to carry her? You need a break."

Adrian rubbed an aching bicep. As he pressed a thumb deeply into the muscle, it loosened a bit, enough to ease the pain. "I'll be all right. Thanks anyway."

Notice that the scene begins with the character's name and describes something he does. This signals readers that they will experience the scene through this character's senses. This kind of beginning is not an essential element of this type of POV, but it is helpful to situate readers.

Through Adrian's senses, readers feel the swirling cold air, the drizzle, and the sweat. Then, through Adrian's eyes, readers see two characters sit and drink falling raindrops.

Like the omniscient option, this POV can allow readers to become intimately acquainted with multiple characters, but only if the author switches POV among those characters. Some stories have a single POV character throughout, while others switch from one POV character to another from time to time.

If an author wants to use this POV and tell a story from multiple viewpoints, it is better to wait for a new scene to switch the viewpoint from one character to another. If the viewpoint switches within a scene, readers might become confused about which character they are seeing the story through.

For example:

> "Want to play chess?" Trudy asked as she set pieces on the board, hoping Greg would say yes. Since she barely knew him, they needed more time together.
>
> "Not today," Greg said. He liked chess, but he hated losing more than anything, and he knew Trudy would destroy him.
>
> "You're a coward," Rosanne called from the kitchen. She smiled. It was time her brother learned a lesson in humility.
>
> "Am not," Greg said. "I just have a headache." That was true enough, but it wasn't the real reason. Unfortunately, Rosanne probably wasn't going to let the subject drop.
>
> "Leave him be," Trudy said. "He had a rough day." She concealed a smile. Maybe now that she gave Greg a break, he might pay more attention to her.

The first perspective was Trudy's. She gave an explanation of why she wanted Greg to play chess with her. Then the perspective changed to Greg's, and we were able to read his mind about his chances of winning the match. After that, we dove into Rosanne's mind to learn her thoughts on the matter, then we switched back to Greg's thoughts again. Finally, we focused on Trudy's thoughts once more to learn why she gave up on the match.

As you can see, this is a lot of POV switching, often called head-hopping, which can be jarring to readers. In short, don't do it.

If a mid-scene switch is absolutely necessary, then show the break with a blank line or a line with only a symbol to let the reader know that a shift is occurring.

As you are writing, if essential mid-scene switches become too common, then consider using omniscient POV instead of third person limited.

Overall, I think third-person-limited POV provides an author with the best balance of intimacy and flexibility, and an author should always avoid switching POV during a scene.

First-person Point of View

First-person is similar to third-person-limited in that the author describes only what the focal character sees, hears, smells, touches, or knows about. With first-person POV, the focal character is the storyteller, and the writer employs first-person pronouns (I, we, us, our) for that character and third-person pronouns for other characters.

For example, here is the beginning of Reapers again:

> The death alarm sounded, that phantom punch in the gut I always dreaded. I touched the metallic gateway valve embedded in my chest at the top of my sternum—warm but not yet hot. The alarm was real. Someone in my territory would die tonight, and I had to find the poor soul. Death didn't care about the late hour. Reapers like me always stayed on call.

Every sensation comes through the "I" character—visuals, feelings, and even thoughts. Stories written in first-person POV usually do not shift to another character throughout the story. The "I" character is the main character and storyteller. If you shift to a different character's POV, it harms the idea that the initial "I" character is the true storyteller. An author needs to have an compelling reason to shift to a different character when using this POV.

For example, an author might want the intimacy of first-person POV, but a crucial part of the action takes place outside the "I" character's perspective. If the best way to tell the story is to communicate that action to the reader in real time, the author might want to tell the vast majority of a story from the "I" character's POV but shift to third-person-limited POV during that scene. It might be better, however, to tell the entire story in third-person-limited POV, but the author has to decide which POV works better overall.

Point of View Intimacy

A major advantage of using third-person-limited POV or first-person POV is the ability to get inside the focal character's skin and show a story through that character's senses. This allows readers to feel as if they are in the story and following the character personally, which enhances reader enjoyment. Some teachers call this "intimate" POV. Others refer to it as DPOV or Deep Point of View.

Here are ways to establish this inside-the-character feeling:

1. **Report only what the focal character sees, hears, feels, smells, tastes, or thinks without using narrator phrases to introduce the sensations.**

Let's explore this method using the following example, the start of a scene from my book Liberator:

> Randall let his gaze drift from a tall evergreen tree to a moss-covered boulder to a marshy pool. The early morning sounds of the forest—cricket chirps, bird calls, and dripping dew—had diminished ... ominously so. Even the breeze had settled, and the treetops no longer rustled. In spite of the still air, leaves fell from the deciduous trees like rain, as if autumn had arrived at an accelerated rate. The loss of shelter was troubling. Soon any beast flying overhead would be able to spot them.

I began the scene with the focal character's name and described something he did, thereby signaling that this character will provide the point of view. In other words, all input will come through Randall's senses.

I avoided typical phrases such as "he saw" or "he heard." Such phrases harm intimacy and draw readers away from being inside a character's head, because they make it sound as if a narrator is relating the sensations rather than the character.

There is no need to write "he saw." Just report the visual. Since Randall is the focal character, readers will know that he saw it. You don't need to write "he heard." If you report the sound, that means the focal character heard it. The same is true with smell, touch, and taste.

Notice that Randall's thoughts are subtly provided. The sounds had diminished "ominously." Who decided that this was ominous? The focal character did. Who compared the falling leaves to rain? Again, the focal character. Who concluded that this leaf-fall episode was like autumn arriving early? Correct. Randall. Who thought the loss of shelter was troubling? You know the answer.

This point is important. I never had to write "he thought" or "he concluded" when communicating thoughts. With intimate, limited POV, readers are deeply embedded in a character's mind, so these thoughts flow with the narrative. Readers become that character and experience the story as if they were in the scene themselves.

Check out these two examples, one written with narrator tags (boldfaced) and one without:

> Signaling for Wallace to follow, Elyssa closed in. **She saw** a heavy chain and an iron manacle that bound the dragon's back leg to the pedestal. **She also noticed** long scratches on his wings and a gouge dividing two scales on his neck. He appeared to have been scourged and then shackled, a prisoner left here alone. But for what purpose? **she thought.**

> Signaling for Wallace to follow, Elyssa closed in. A heavy chain and an iron manacle bound the dragon's back leg to the pedestal. Long scratches covered his wings, and a gouge divided two scales on his neck. He appeared to have been scourged and then shackled, a prisoner left here alone, but for what purpose?

I trust that you can perceive which one feels more inside Elyssa's head. The second one provided her visuals and thoughts without narrator intrusion. Readers see through her eyes and read her mind's conclusion, making them feel present in the scene.

2. Avoid describing anything that the focal character cannot perceive or would not notice.

In limited POV, whether third person or first person, don't tell readers what the focal character cannot take in with his own senses. The character doesn't see what's going on in a different room, though he might hear sounds and draw a conclusion based on the audible input. With the exception of mind-reading characters, the focal character doesn't know someone else's thoughts, though facial expressions or body language can give him an idea.

Many writers correctly employ this concept, but some miss a subtler issue. When writing intimate point of view, it is not the best practice to report details in a scene, or personal physical qualities, that a character wouldn't normally notice.

For example, when most people walk into their own bedrooms, they normally don't notice the color of the walls, the texture of the carpet, or how high the ceiling is. They have been there so many times, these details are not an issue. It would be odd to mentally register what we wouldn't notice.

The same is true with details about ourselves. If we comb our fingers through our hair, we wouldn't think about its color or how curly it is unless something has changed recently. Yet, many writers report these details without giving thought to the fact that their characters probably didn't notice them.

Details like these harm intimacy and disturb the illusion of realism we're hoping to create. When a writer reports a mundane detail, readers might not consciously register the lack of realism, but the illusion might become fractured anyway.

Most mundane details are not important to a scene, so in many cases you can just avoid reporting them. But if the details enhance the story or the world-building you hope to establish, you can include them by attracting the character's attention to the details in a natural way.

For example, if you want to describe a tree in a character's front yard, have a bird fly into a nest in the branches. This will cause the character to look and perhaps take in the tree's foliage, how its thickness hides the nest well. If you want the character to notice his wife's hair, have her enter the scene with a fresh cut or a new color.

To illustrate this concept, let's look at an excerpt from a piece an aspiring writer sent to me:

> After a few more turns the gravel path beneath her feet turned into the familiar paved streets of the main square. As the sky grew lighter she could see her destination, dark and foreboding, just two hundred yards distant.
>
> The council's building loomed like death's shadow at the end of the cobblestone lane. The large gate to the courtyard would be locked and guarded, as the sun hadn't risen yet. The granite columns, which surrounded the building while providing anchor points for the perimeter fence, were definitely the most impressive feature of the complex.
>
> While all twelve held designs, the two that stood front and center were the most magnificent of them all. Each one was carved with designs of dragons of all sizes and colors. The mere sight of

them was enough to chase away her foul mood. Perhaps the morning wouldn't be as bad as she had thought.

The focal character has seen this structure many times, so it's odd that she would take such careful note of it. To her, it's the same old thing.

When I want to describe something like this, I will have a character notice a change of some kind so that her attention is drawn not only to the change but also to the rest of the structure. Then she can check to see if anything else has changed. Also, I would try to add more clarity to the visuals and *show* her change of mood rather than *tell* about it. (More on showing versus telling starting on page 180.)

> After a few more turns the gravel path gave way to the main square's familiar cobblestone streets. As the sky grew lighter, her destination came into view, dark and foreboding, just two hundred yards distant. The council's building loomed like death's shadow at the end of the lane.
>
> She walked on, head low, shoulders sagging. Losing was bad enough, but facing the council members? Their sharp tongues would show no mercy.
>
> When she arrived at the gate, a pebble dropped and rolled to her boot. She looked up and scanned the barrier, trying to locate the source. Might there be

a fault in one of the granite columns surrounding the building? They had always provided anchor points for the perimeter fence, so they needed to be strong and impenetrable.

She let her gaze pass across the twelve columns and their designs. The two at the front, each bearing the carving of a red dragon in flight, seemed intact, as did the lesser dragons on the other columns, whether blue, green, or orange.

As she stared at the magnificent creatures, she inhaled deeply. What beauty! What inspiration! How many times had she passed by these columns without taking a second glance?

She picked up the pebble, slid it into her pocket, and squared her shoulders. The training defeat today was the mere dropping of a pebble. The columns, and her determination, had lost nothing of consequence. She would press on, no matter what.

The falling of a pebble drew her attention to the details and allowed for a natural way to describe the beauty. It's also natural for a character to take wonder in the fact that such details had escaped notice before. Many people let amazing beauty pass by because they're too busy to pay attention.

Using methods like this, you can describe familiar objects, but what about familiar people, that is, other characters the focal character knows well?

When you come upon someone you see every day, how often do you take notice of that person's eye color, nose shape, hairstyle, etc? If you're like most people, probably not often, perhaps only when something happens that highlights the feature—the person gets a radical haircut, breaks her nose, or wears glasses for the first time.

How do you describe a character the POV character sees frequently? By coming up with ways for the POV character to take notice—an unusual angle for light to strike the character; problems with clothing, such as stains or rips; misaligned hair; bloodshot eyes; or an altered state of consciousness, perhaps induced by sleepiness, medication, etc.

In *Beyond the Gateway*, the sequel to *Reapers*, here is how Phoenix sees Shanghai, his notice sparked by her battle-weary appearance:

> Shanghai stood next to me below my apartment. Early morning sun shone on her from the alley opening. The light revealed rips and bloodstains at the elbows and knees of her Reaper ensemble—forest green pants; black shirt and running shoes; and cloak, its hood pulled back, revealing an oozing gash on her forehead. The damage, along with the surrounding broken beer bottles and other alley trash, made her look like she had been in a bar brawl.

The next time he takes special notice of her, his consciousness has been altered by an energy charge, putting him in a euphoric state:

> Although dirt marred her Asian features from chin to scalp, and tangles mussed her ebony hair, she radiated beauty from the top of her lovely head, down her athletic, toned body, to her sleek legs. She was the model of feminine perfection.

Describing the POV character can be even more difficult. If the character isn't aware of any of his own appearance changes, no physical descriptions would come through that character's sensory input.

Many writers use what is sometimes called the "mirror trick," that is, the character looks in a mirror, giving the writer an opportunity to tell the reader the character's physical traits. The first problem with that method: unless there is a compelling reason for the character to look at a mirror, experienced readers will recognize this as a trick. In other words, if you want to use the mirror trick, you need a reasonable motivation for the character to check his or her reflection, perhaps to examine a bleeding wound or to try to get a foreign object out of an eye.

The second problem: even when looking at a mirror, a character wouldn't usually notice the details that he or she has seen thousands of times. In order to report them, you might have to employ some of the same methods I mentioned above—bloodshot eyes, misaligned hair, etc.

Hair wetness can cause a character to notice that her hair is a darker shade of brown than usual. New clothing can have bright colors that cause a notice of matching eye color. Exhaustion and thirst can raise awareness of cracked or dry lips.

If, however, you are not trying to employ an intimate point of view, you need not be concerned about these issues. Go ahead and say that the character has brown hair, blue eyes, and stands six feet tall. It's a lot easier. Yet, although intimate point of view is far more difficult, it yields a huge benefit—putting readers inside the skin of the POV character, which results in a more emotionally impactful, intense, and thrilling experience. When we "Write them In," readers enjoy the journey at a far deeper level.

3. Dive deeply into the character's mind to explore his or her thoughts and emotions.

For readers, knowing what a character is thinking is the utmost in intimate experience. Thoughts, feelings, moods, regrets about the past, and plans for the future might never be spoken. Readers need a journey through a character's mind to learn the secrets of hidden motivations. Without knowing the motivations for a character's actions, readers would miss out on the most powerful aspect of the journey—the passions and motivations that drive the character ever onward toward the story's goal.

When you write with intimate POV, whenever the focal character does anything, readers must know why the character did it before you report the action. If readers don't find out the reason until after they read the action, then you have harmed intimacy.

It's sometimes difficult for an author to dive into a character's mind in a way that doesn't shake or confuse readers. During a scene, an author might be describing what is going on around the character, reported through the character's sensory input of external surroundings, then the author jumps to describing the character's thoughts without a transition. It's a sudden leap from the external to the internal, which can feel like a jolt.

The solution is to include an external-to-internal transition by writing an action for the focal character so readers are drawn to him and away from focusing on what is surrounding him.

For example, from my book *Warrior*:

> As she imagined shards scattering across the floor, she looked at the dragon's face. His visage brightened, as if his heart were tied to the crystal's energy—an odd response to pain.
>
> Elyssa returned her gaze to the sphere. What did this peculiar torture device mean to the dragons? With its prominent placement in the observatory, it had to be more than a lie detector. It was a treasure, perhaps even an object of worship. And that made it a point of vulnerability.
>
> Grimacing as the pain increased, Elyssa reared back with the blade, ready to strike. "You will take us to Jason, or I'll smash your precious crystal!"

In Elyssa's POV, she is thinking about the floor and the dragon. Before that, the scene provided more descriptions of what Elyssa saw in this observatory, which included a glowing crystalline sphere sitting on a pedestal at the center of the room. It emitted light that stung anyone standing in its radiance. Also, it brightened if someone told the truth and darkened if someone told a lie, making it a lie detector.

In addition, the dragon has refused to lead Elyssa to her friend Jason, and she's trying to figure out a way to get him to acquiesce to her request.

While taking in the description, readers are focused on what is external to Elyssa—the observatory and the sphere. After writing that description, I wanted to let readers know her thoughts about what she saw. I needed a transition to draw readers back to Elyssa before diving into her thoughts. I did this by providing Elyssa with an action that focused on her and the topic she was going to think about—"Elyssa returned her gaze to the sphere."

This phrase brings readers from the larger setting, including the floor and the dragon immediately before that sentence, to Elyssa herself, making it clear that the question and comments that follow are her thoughts. She ponders the sphere, analyzes its purposes, and comes to a conclusion that it is a vulnerability point she can exploit. This description of her thoughts is called Interior Monologue (IM). (More about that topic beginning on page 174.)

The conclusion she draws becomes a motivation for her next action, to threaten to attack the sphere as a way of forcing the dragon to do as she requested.

Without the ability to dive into Elyssa's thoughts and experience her IM, readers would not have a clear understanding as to why she chose to attack the sphere. Being able to read her thoughts puts readers inside her head, thereby establishing close intimacy. Readers sense everything she does, including the thinking process that drives her actions.

Remember, the key to allowing readers to know who is expressing thoughts is a transitional phrase, a personal action that draws readers to the character. Also, it's often a good idea to have a character follow a similar pattern of thought, as follows:

1. **A question about what is seen, heard, or smelled.**
2. **An analysis that adds to a character's knowledge and experience.**
3. **A conclusion that creates a motivation for the character's next action.**

One more item to take into account: A dive into a character's mind should take place during a pause in the action when the character has time to think or reflect. Avoid IM episodes when intense action is going on.

Let's look at another example that demonstrates a different purpose of thought intimacy—letting readers see how a character tries to figure out a complicated situation that includes history, analysis, and suspicions.

Writing such a thought process can be challenging, as one writer declared when he presented me with the following paragraph, asking how to improve it with regard to point-of-view, intimacy, and how to handle pronouns and their antecedents.

In this passage, Wraith and Ellis are both male, and Edge is Female. Edge is the POV character.

> Wraith's plan was simple, as all good plans are, but Edge still didn't like it. The final member of their party was a low-level data processor named Arthur Ellis. Ellis was currently living under an assumed name and toiling in the obscurity of the working class. Wraith didn't explain why Ellis changed his name or even what it was now, but he gave her a current image of the man and wanted him abducted from his home in Lennox Heights. That was the part of the plan she didn't like.

The paragraph begins with Edge's thoughts (Wraith's plan was simple), but at this point, readers might not be sure of who is generating that thought. When we read "Edge didn't like it," then we get an idea that these might be Edge's thoughts, but that idea might also come from a third person or even a narrator.

When the first clue to identifying the POV sounds like a narrator, the rest of the paragraph can come across as narrated rather than a flow of the character's thinking process. The conclusion, "That was the part of the plan she didn't like," feels like a narrator's conclusion instead of Edge's.

Here is my suggested rewrite:

> Edge set a fist on her hip. Wraith's plan was simple, as all good plans are, but it still lacked something. What could it be? The weak link might be Arthur Ellis, a low-level data processor living under an assumed name–a grunt toiling in working-class obscurity. Wraith never explained why Ellis changed his name or even what it was now, choosing only to supply her with a photo image of Ellis as well as instructions to abduct him from his home in Lennox Heights. That part of the plan stunk. Too much mystery.

The opening sentence gives Edge a transitional action that draws readers to her. It sets her in a thinking posture, which indicates that the next sentence will contain her thoughts. The plan lacked something that she couldn't put her finger on, and she raised the question "What could it be?"

The rest of the paragraph shows her analyzing the question in a natural way. As she ponders the details, she gives a bit of back-story history and comes to a conclusion that sounds like internal thought in the character's voice instead of a narrator's assigned conclusion. "That part of the plan stunk" doesn't sound like it comes from a narrator.

The natural thinking process also helps to clear up which pronouns belong to which antecedents, thereby making the entire paragraph easy to read and understand.

Also, the transitional action (Edge set a fist on her hip) provides an opportunity to show the character's emotions, mindset, or mood. A fist on the hip, especially for a woman, communicates anger or frustration. A man often clenches a fist or sets his jaw. Scratching the head communicates confusion, slumping shoulders can mean exhaustion or disappointment, and biting the lip often indicates pensiveness. Whichever mindset you choose, be sure to write the thought process in a way that reflects that mood.

Here is a key to avoiding the feel of narrator intrusion: As often as possible, use the name of your POV character only when narrating action. "Edge set a fist on her hip" is action. "Edge still didn't like it" is not action; it is the telling of a thought by a narrator.

The same is true with pronouns that refer to the POV character. "That's the part of the plan she didn't like" is not action. Instead I suggested "That part of the plan stunk," which removes the pronoun. Readers know that Edge is thinking this, because she is the focal character. The phrase I added, that the idea stunk, shows that she didn't like the idea. Simply telling the reader she didn't like it sounds like a narrator's conclusion.

In summary, start with a transitional phrase that indicates a character's thoughts are about to follow. Then allow the character to go through the thought process in a natural way that sounds like the character's voice. By doing this, readers will ride along with the thinking process without believing that a narrator is telling them the thoughts.

These examples have provided short glimpses into a character's mind in order to reveal thoughts and motivations. They were shallow dives rather than deep plunges.

In order to fully connect readers with a character, it is helpful to occasionally take a deeper dive and explore the character's hopes, dreams, fears, and doubts. These plunges also allow you to develop your story's theme by raising important issues in the character's mind, slowly bringing them to the surface through the story's conflicts—themes like sacrifice, courage, forgiveness, mercy, or whatever the character might be dealing with on a personal level.

Such explorations need to come during a rest period in the story, that is, after a conflict and before the next. Allow the character time to reflect on what happened in the previous conflict—what he or she might have done right or wrong—and allow these successes or failures to factor into the thoughts.

For example, in *Reapers,*:

> I let out a quiet sigh. The winds of change blow through every life, sometimes with a ferocity no one can predict. I could keep my promise to wait for Misty. My life as a Reaper demanded solitude. But Misty had likely met plenty of attractive young men who would love to ease her loneliness. Maybe her pewter ring soon felt like a lead weight, and the words of promise took on the tone of childish hope. When she realized the limitations of our youthful vision, maybe the loss of blinders led her to remove the pewter shackle and deposit it in a jewelry box, a place for shiny baubles

and pretty keepsakes ... and a coffin for our dreams.

I curled my fingers, feeling the tightness of the ring. A new weight of reality burdened my heart. I had learned so much in three short years ... too much, really. Visions of death and grief do that to every Reaper. We grow into adults before our time, and solitude provides too many hours to reflect and ponder. In only a few years, Reapers become poets, mentally writing bitter verses that reflect bitter hearts.

I brought the ring to my cheek and rubbed the cool metal against my skin. No matter what Misty did, I would keep my promise. I couldn't let those bitter winds infect my heart. Although Sing and Shanghai were both beautiful young women inside and out, giving in to their charms would break my only attachment to the days when love still thrived through any storm—days of innocent ignorance, to be sure, but days when I looked forward to each coming dawn. If I broke that connection, all hope that those days might return would be shattered forever.

Without this deep dive, readers wouldn't be able to understand Phoenix's heartaches, the motivations that drive him. The dive also exposes his deep-seated bitterness toward his station in life, forced servitude as a Reaper. Yet, he still does his job. Why? Because he is a loving person, a sacrificial hero.

When readers see this quality, that Phoenix refuses to allow the past to embitter his soul to the point of apathy, they will love him for it, they will cheer for him all the more, and they will ride with him on his inner journey. This is a crucial component in getting readers to love your story.

Tool #2 - Motivation/Reaction Units

Motivation/Reaction Units (M-R Units) are cause-and-effect sequences in a story that show a cycle of cause (motivation), then effect (reaction), and the effect becomes the cause for the next effect and so on.

The foundation of this technique is simple—every action, word, or thought that you write for a point-of-view character should have a reasonably clear motivation, that is, readers have a good idea of why the character acted, whether in thought, word, or deed. Since readers are supposed to be inside the skin of the character, they should know why the character does anything at the moment the action occurs. Nothing should be hidden.

First rule of this technique: Motivation precedes reaction. Readers should know the character's reason for any action before reading the action. For example, the following is wrongly stated:

Misty cringed when the dog barked.

"Misty cringed" is the action (or reaction). The dog barking is the motivation for her action. Since the dog barking was the motivation and occurred first, it should be reported first, because when readers see "Misty cringed," for a moment they don't know why she cringed. If they are inside her skin, as they should be, they would know why. For one brief moment they are blinded to the reason for her action, and they lose intimacy.

More examples:

Incorrect: He arched his back and cried for mercy as electricity shot through his body, running up and down his spine.

Correct: Electricity shot through his body, running up and down his spine. He arched his back and cried for mercy.

Incorrect: His head cracked on the floor once more as another jolt shook him, and blackness overcame all his senses.

Correct: As another jolt shook him, his head cracked on the floor once more, and blackness overcame all his senses.

When characters react to motivations, their reactions are usually one or more of the following: An involuntary action, a voluntary action, or speech (spoken aloud or as thoughts). Sometimes a character will react in only one of these ways, sometimes two, and sometimes all three. Whenever a character reacts in more than one of these ways, the most natural sequential order is as listed above. Involuntary action usually precedes voluntary action or speech, and voluntary action usually precedes speech.

For example: The Doberman snarled. Her legs shaking, Misty ducked behind a skinny tree and cried out, "Help me!"

Misty reacted first with shaking legs (involuntary), then by ducking behind a tree (voluntary), then by crying out. This order of reactions doesn't always hold true, but it is the most natural progression, and it will feel right to readers.

When a character faces danger, involuntary reactions can include cringing, ducking out of the way, striking with a fist, or even shouting (though often not with words)—anything that a character would do without consciously thinking about it. These are knee-jerk reactions.

Voluntary reactions include hiding in the cellar, loading a gun, searching for an escape route, or anything that requires conscious thought.

And, of course, reactions differ greatly depending on the kind of stimuli that cause them.

For characters who are not the POV character, readers will often not know what motivates them, because readers are not inside their skin. Yet, readers should always understand, without exception, why the POV character does anything, even if the reason appears to be foolish or ill-advised (in the readers' minds).

Like dominoes falling in a line, your story should be a long series of Motivation/Reaction Units. Every action, whether physical, spoken, or thought should be a reaction to something that happened in a recent sentence or paragraph, and that reaction transforms into the motivation for the next reaction.

Let's look at a lengthy excerpt from *Reapers* to illustrate a long sequence of these M-R Units. Comments are in bold.

Molly choked on the pills and coughed them up. **(Reaction to family trying to force feed the pills, not shown.)** Her body stiffened, and she let out a moan. **(Reaction to not taking the medicine.)** While the three patted her hands and stroked her head in futility. **(Reaction to her moan.)** I swallowed hard. Even after more than three years as a Reaper, the sight of a dying child still tore a hole in my heart. **(Reaction to all of the above.)**

My cloak vibrated, sending hot prickles across my arms. **(A Reaper's reaction to impending death.)** The end was near. Only one hope remained—the syringe. **(Reaction in thought process.)**

As I reached into my pocket **(Reaction to thinking about the syringe.)**, the rusty hinges at the front door squeaked. Everyone froze. Fiona whispered, "I heard no knock." **(Reactions to the door squeaking.)**

Colm shoved the pill bottle into his pocket. Fiona and Colleen rose and backed away from the bed, their eyes wide with fear. **(Reactions to someone coming in the door.)** Molly's body loosened, and she breathed in gasping spasms.

The bedroom door swung open. **(A new**

action that has no apparent motivation, but we find out later why she has come.) A tall woman dressed in black leather stepped in and scanned the room. Piercing gray eyes set beneath a somber brow gave her the aspect of a bird of prey searching for a victim. With youthful face, trim body, and blonde hair draped over her shoulders, she looked nothing like the steroid-jacked male officer who normally patrolled at night. Yet, the leather pants and jacket with a Gateway insignia on the left breast pocket confirmed her status as a death officer of some kind. **(Phoenix's observations are a reaction to her entry.)**

Her shifting gaze halted at Molly. "A young one," she said in a low monotone. "My condolences." **(The woman's reactions to Molly's travail.)**

I withdrew my hand from my pocket. **(Reaction to the woman coming in. He can't reveal the syringe now.)** and, forcing an emotionally detached countenance, crouched next to the bed. "She's still alive, though the end is near." **(Reaction to her words. He has to go into Reaper mode.)**

"Quite near." **(Reaction to Phoenix's words.)** The officer sat on the bed and stroked Molly's hair. Her hand trembled as her fingers passed over the little girl's locks again and again. "Such a beautiful princess. She will be a glittering star in the heavens. I am looking forward to seeing her drawn away from this broken shell so she can be set free to brighten the skies." **(The woman's further reactions to Molly's impending death.)**

The family's terrified expressions shouted urgency. **(Family's reaction to the woman's actions.)** Somehow I had to get rid of this officer so we could try to save Molly. **(Phoenix's reaction to the woman's actions.)**

I touched the officer's arm. "Because of this child's age and the high potential for extraction pangs, the reaping will cause an emotional upheaval, so if you wouldn't mind sitting in the front room, I will withdraw her soul in private and call you when—" **(Phoenix's reaction to what the woman is doing.)**

"Heightened emotions are normal and expected." She unzipped her jacket, revealing a form-fitting white T-shirt and a gun in a shoulder holster. "Pain is normal. Weeping is a necessary catharsis." **(The woman's reactions to Phoenix's actions.)**

I drew back. "I suppose that's true,

but—" (**Phoenix's reaction to seeing the gun.**)

"My name is Alex." She extended her hand, though her expression remained stern. "And you're Phoenix." (**Alex's reaction to Phoenix's sudden fear.**)

"That's right." I shook her hand, again not bothering to ask how a stranger knew my name. "I guess you're not familiar with customary reaping procedures. Since the family requests privacy …" (**Phoenix's reactions to Alex extending her hand.**)

"Familiar?" Anger flickered in her eyes. (**Alex's reaction to Phoenix's words.**) "I attended reapings before you were born, and I have followed your career ever since—" Her brow furrowing (**Here we see Alex's reaction to finding a pill before seeing the motivation for it, because she is not the POV character. Phoenix, who is the POV character, sees the furrowed brow before he notices why her brow furrows, so this is in the proper order.**), she picked up a pill from the mattress. "What is this?"

"Candy," I said without hesitating. "I always bring some when a dying child has siblings. Molly has two sisters."

(Phoenix's reaction to Alex's discovery of the pill.)

Notice that each reaction becomes a motivation for the next reaction, thereby setting up linked chains. The links in the chain are the motivation/reaction units, and the M-R Units continue occurring, one after another after another. Everything happens for a reason, and when the units come in an unbroken series, readers feel like they are in the room while events are happening. Readers are never "out of the loop."

Writing these units in the proper way, however, can become obsessive. It's important to remember that clear writing that helps us tell our stories is more important than the motivation-reaction principles.

Look at this example:

> He stopped the flashlight beam on a battery lamp, sat on the floor next to it, and turned it on, keeping it at a low level to save power.

In the strictest sense, this example has two out-of-order motivation-reaction sequences.

1. He stopped the flashlight beam because it came across the lamp, but the text reports the stopping before mentioning the lamp. Readers don't know the motivation for stopping until after the action. That's out of order.

2. The reason for keeping the lamp at a low level is to save power. Therefore, to follow the M/R order perfectly, the writer should mention the motivation of

saving power before the reaction, that is, keeping the lamp at a low level.

Since the motivations come immediately after the reactions, only a little harm to POV intimacy is likely. If the writer has difficulty figuring out how to alter the order without making the phrasing awkward, then it might be better to leave it alone. In other words, don't obsess over this principle.

Still, if you want to avoid any loss of intimacy, you can probably find a way to rewrite a paragraph to keep the motivation/reaction sequence in the proper order.

Here is one way to do so with the example:

> He swept the beam across a battery-powered lamp. "Ah. This will help. No idea how long it's been here, though." He sat on the floor next to the lamp and turned it on at a low level. The dim glow illuminated the cavern, allowing him to flick his penlight off.

Since there is no mention of stopping the beam, that out-of-order phrase is no longer an issue. Also, his mention of wondering how long the lamp's been there implies that he's concerned that it might not work, giving reason for turning it on at a low level, which sets the motivation and reaction in their proper order.

To master this writing tool, I highly recommend reading *Techniques of the Selling Writer* by Dwight V. Swain. Among other vital issues, he goes into detail about M-R units, concluding with:

> Writers ... will recognize the M-R unit

for what it is: a tool, infinitely valuable, whose use they must master so completely that its skilled manipulation becomes automatic and instinctive. ... How do you least painfully achieve such mastery? ... To write in whatever manner comes easiest for you, paying no attention to any rules whatever. Then, go back over your copy and check to make sure that each reaction is motivated; that each motivating stimulus gets a reaction; and that ineptitude in use of language has not in any way confused the issue.[1]

Practice will make this skill seem like second nature. You will begin seeing unmotivated actions as if they were warning lights. A strong motivation that lacks a reaction will seem like a lost orphan begging to be noticed. Broken links in M-R unit chains will appear to be gaping holes that demand transitions.

Also, you will recognize that you have applied this tool correctly when you try to insert something new in an earlier part of your story, such as a foreshadowing element, and you can't find a place to put it because the insertion will break an M-R unit link. Congratulations. Your M-R chain is strong.

---

1   Dwight V. Swain, *Techniques of the Selling Writer*, (University of Oklahoma Press, 1973), 82.

Tool #3 - Narrative

Narrative is a collection of descriptions of scenes and actions, one of the three major vehicles used in storytelling:

Dialogue - The characters talk, explaining their thoughts.

Interior Monologue - A character thinks, explaining what's going on inside his head.

Narrative - Pretty much everything else.

In narrative, the author explains what is going on, often through the sensory input of a character. When you employ an intimate point of view, it feels like the character becomes the narrator.

To illustrate, let's break down the sentences in the following paragraph:

(1) I sat on my bed tapping on my laptop computer while Clara peered out the window. (2) She was being paranoid again. (3) The Mustang driver who followed us to the motel had really spooked her. (4) "Chill out, Clara. He can't possibly guess where we are."

1. Narrative: Explains what is going on. The narrator is the "I" character instead of the author.

2. Interior monologue: Explains what the "I" character is thinking.
3. Interior monologue.
4. Dialogue.

Here is another example:

> I pushed the laptop to the side, slid out of the bed, and looked over Clara's shoulder. The Mustang sat parked under a tree, the driver watching the motel's front door. An intermittent shower of leaves, blown around by Chicago's never-ending breezes, danced about on the convertible's ragtop. "He's not Colombian, Clara. He's Middle Eastern."

In this case, all but the last sentence is narrative. Notice that every description and action is reported through the eyes of the point-of-view (POV) character, making him the narrator. These sentences describe what the character sees, not necessarily what the character thinks about the visuals.

Yet, in intimate POV, narrative and interior monologue can often blur. In this example, the character inserted "never-ending" because of his experiences in Chicago. He doesn't actually see "never-ending" at this moment, so the sentence isn't pure narrative. It is a blend of narrative and character commentary.

This character narration and blurring is especially evident in first-person POV, but an intimate third-person-limited POV narrative can achieve the same results. Here is the same paragraph rewritten in third-person, limited:

> Nathan pushed the laptop to the side, slid out of the bed, and looked over Clara's shoulder. The Mustang sat parked under a tree, the driver watching the motel's front door. An intermittent shower of leaves, blown around by Chicago's never-ending breezes, danced about on the convertible's ragtop. "He's not Colombian, Clara. He's Middle Eastern."

Only one word changed: "I" became "Nathan." He is still the narrator, and every part of the narrative comes through his sensory input, including his observation that the breezes are never-ending.

In omniscient POV however, the author is the narrator. While using this POV, an author might insert opinions, historical facts, or other observations. This practice of including insertions is not popular at this time and is often derisively called "author intrusion."

Here is a classic example of omniscient POV narrative from *A Tale of Two Cities* by Charles Dickens:

> It was the best of times, it was the worst of times, it was the age of wisdom, it was the age of foolishness, it was the epoch of belief, it was the epoch of incredulity, it was the season of Light, it was the season of Darkness, it was the spring of hope, it was the winter of despair, we had everything before us, we had nothing before us, we were all going direct to Heaven, we were all going direct the

> other way--in short, the period was so far like the present period, that some of its noisiest authorities insisted on its being received, for good or for evil, in the superlative degree of comparison only.

This is filled with the author's observations and opinions. No story character could have provided this insight.

When you write narrative, you are usually simply describing the action taking place, but be careful to avoid providing every detail. This is called stage direction.

For example, when a character opens a door, you don't have to explain that he grasps the doorknob with his right hand and turns the knob. Most readers will assume that. Just report that he opens the door. Readers will fill in the gaps.

If the detail is important for the story, however, leave it in. Sometimes turning the knob can add tension as the character thinks about what dangers might be lurking beyond the door, or maybe the knob is hot, telling the character that a fire awaits on the other side.

In the two paragraphs below, the first is an example of stage direction, while the second takes out the actions that readers will assume.

> Johnny dropped the sword to the ground three feet away and lowered himself to his right knee next to Martin's left hip. He dug his right index finger between Martin's shirt buttons, pulled

one part of the shirt to the left, popping buttons in the process, and searched Martin from the top of his collar bone to his waist, trying to find the deadly bee sting. Once he found it, he withdrew the tube of healing ointment from the leather pouch on his belt, unscrewed the cap, and squeezed out about a teaspoon of the grayish goop on his left index finger, then applied it to the sting, spreading it around in a circle with a radius of about three inches.

Johnny dropped the sword, knelt at Martin's side, and ripped his shirt open. After finding the sting, he grabbed the ointment tube from his belt and rubbed a dollop of salve on the wound in a widening swirl.

Leaving out unnecessary details is especially important when writing action scenes. Each detail you include slows the pace. Before the action begins, set the scene with all of the necessary descriptions. Then when the action begins, readers will have the setting in mind, and the action can take place on that mental stage without a lot of new details.

Save your detailed descriptions for slow, contemplative scenes, such as in rest periods. Employ longer sentences and include colors, textures, etc. This creates a meditative mood that will allow you to dive into the character's thoughts through interior monologue.

Also, be sure to maintain proper proportions. In

your narrative, don't spend a lot of time on minor issues. Don't cut important scenes too short. If solving a character's personal issues leads to the resolution of a conflict, then spend more time on the issues. If a cool device invented through a character's intelligence and creativity saves the day, then write more about those attributes and how they developed.

In short, if something is important to the story, focus on it. If not, either mention it in passing or leave it out all together.

Ten Qualities of Good Narrative

1. Provide a goal for the scene.

What is the character's objective? Here again are the first three paragraphs from *Precisely Terminated* by Amanda L. Davis.

> How nice it must be to sleep so peacefully when doom awaited at dawn. Letting out a sigh, Faye pulled a threadbare blanket from a top bunk and surveyed the many beds and sleeping bodies lined up in the cramped room. How little they all knew, these poor, ignorant laborers. Perhaps they would die unaware of the tragedy about to befall them.
>
> As she folded the blanket and laid it back on the bed, a tear welled in her eye. Why did it have to happen this way? She was only a nursemaid, one slave in the midst of thousands. Why should she die because of one man's actions? It simply

> wasn't fair. No, it was cruel, inhumane, tragic ... evil.
>
> She slowly clenched a fist. Fair or unfair, the time had come. The plan had to proceed.

Readers learn early on that Faye has a plan that has to proceed. The details of that plan clarify as the action proceeds. If a scene is not the first one in the story, it should begin with a reminder of what the focal character wants to do, and it should end with an understanding of whether or not the character has achieved that goal. Maybe she has. Maybe she hasn't. Or maybe the goal has changed or pursuing it has been delayed. Whatever the outcome, readers need to know about it before the scene ends.

2. **Establish viewpoint, time, place, and circumstance or goal at the start of every scene. Also add a light source, such as a veiled moon, a flashlight, or a lantern, if the setting would otherwise be dark.**

Once again, here are the first two paragraphs in *Reapers*:

> The death alarm sounded, that phantom punch in the gut I always dreaded. I touched the metallic gateway valve embedded in my chest at the top of my sternum—warm but not yet hot. The alarm was real. Someone in my territory would die tonight, and I had to find the poor soul. Death didn't care about the

late hour. Reapers like me always stayed on call.

I rose from my moth-eaten reading chair, blew out the hanging lantern's flame, and stalked across my one-room apartment to the window, guided by light from outside. The internal alarm grew stronger. Prickly vibrations raced along my cloak from the baggy sleeves to the top of the hood, tickling the two-day stubble across my cheeks and chin. Time was growing short—probably less than an hour left.

Point of View: The "I" character, a Reaper, who becomes more defined later.
The time: It's a late hour.
The place: The character's apartment.
The circumstance or goal: Someone in my territory would die tonight, and I had to find the poor soul.
Light source: A lantern's flame, then light from outside.

3. **Cap off a scene with a curtain line—a focused ending that makes the reader hope for the scene to continue.**

Here is the last paragraph in chapter one of Reapers:

"Very good." Trying to keep my hands steady, I slid the photo stick into my pocket and fished out the pill bottle. "Let's see what we can do for Molly."

The goal was set at the beginning of the scene, to find the poor soul who was about to die. Phoenix finds her, and now he will try to save her. It's called a curtain line, because, like on a theater stage, the curtain drops, metaphorically instead of literally. Readers are left wondering. What will happen next? They want to know. They won't stop reading. Then, in the next scene, Phoenix's goal is not to find her but to save her.

The following is another scene's curtain line from *Reapers*:

> I let my gaze drift to her chest. The chain led behind her tunic, the medallion now hidden from sight. Farther down, her hands lay folded in her lap. The dream provided a good reminder—Sing was really a lonely orphan. Tragic circumstances threw her into this dangerous job against her will and after only a year and a half of training. No wonder she didn't know all the tricks of the trade, and no wonder she was so nervous about rule breaking and intimate contact. She was just trying to survive.
>
> After taking a deep breath, I shut my eyes and nestled closer to her. In spite of the rules and my flatline ways, I would be her friend. From now on that would be my sacred duty, and nothing could keep me from fulfilling it.

The ending sentence can be a conclusion that spikes emotions or an introduction to an intense action scene, anything that closes the previous moment and opens thoughts about an upcoming moment. It is a combination of realization and anticipation. It makes readers glad they read your amazing scene, and it infuses a desire to read the next one. You should strive to accomplish this with every scene.

4. Avoid describing lack of action.

Lack of action: "He couldn't find a bathroom anywhere." Action: "He flung open door after door. No bathroom!"

Lack of action: "He didn't move." Action: "He froze in place."

This is not a hard-and-fast rule. Sometimes lack of action is more profound than action. If a powerful force comes against a character, "He didn't budge" might work better than "He planted his feet."

The key to this narrative quality is to watch for instances where inaction can be better written as action.

5. Keep the tension high.

Your character should be in some kind of "danger" at all times.

Danger shouldn't be released by accident or coincidence. It should be vanquished by the character's actions in a way that shows that he deserves to win.

If something happens that resolves one danger, immediately switch focus to another. If all dangers are alleviated, then add a new one.

6. The beginning of your story should include both mystery and immediate tension.

Read the Ordinary World section in this book for details on this topic.

7. Particular is usually better than general.

For example, use "Tennessee Walker" instead of "horse" and "the six maples" instead of "those trees."

An exception to this advice: Being specific is more visual and paints a better picture, but if your point-of-view character wouldn't identify the specifics because he isn't that sort of person, then use the general term.

For some people, a tree is a tree is a tree. Others would differentiate between a pine and an oak. And a few would call a tree by its scientific name and think about how common or rare it is to find it in that region.

Simply put, be specific as often as you can, that is, whenever it fits your character's ways.

8. Use active verbs as often as possible.

Verbs that show the subject actually doing something are better than static, state-of-being verbs such as "is," "was," and "were."

Here is an exercise that might help you apply this principle. Print the first few pages of your manuscript and use a red marker to circle all uses of "was" and "were" (Or "is" and "are" if you are writing in present tense). Most new writers will find far too many and will be surprised at the frequency. These are opportunities to make the verb phrases more active and vivid.

Also, "was" and "were" are often signs of passive

voice, that is, the subject is not actually doing the action. The action is being done to the subject.

Here is an example of passive voice:

Bill was swarmed by a massive army of mosquitoes.

This is passive voice, because Bill is the subject, and he isn't the one doing the verb (swarmed). He is passive.

In most cases, it is better to alter the sentence to an active state.

A massive army of mosquitoes swarmed Bill.

The subject is now the noun that actually did the verb.

This changing of voice is also not a hard-and-fast rule. Sometimes passive voice is the better option, especially when the character's passivity is important.

For example: "He was insulted, tortured, and maimed, but he said not a word.

Consider each use of was or were as a potential opportunity to improve a sentence by using a more vivid verb or switching from passive to active voice. Not every case will need a change, but they are all worth looking into.

9. **Make sure your pronoun antecedents are clear and correct.**

> Frank and Jim ran to the ladder. When they arrived, he offered him a hand.

Who offered whom a hand? It's impossible to tell.

> He scanned the raised hands for a volunteer. They would have to be someone strong and brave.

"Volunteer" is singular, but "they" is plural, so the pronoun, they, doesn't match the antecedent noun, volunteer.

Using "they" or "them" as singular pronouns has gained acceptance of late, but following this practice can cause confusion, which is why I advise against it.

10. Look for paragraphs that begin the same way more than a couple of times consecutively.

Do four paragraphs in a row begin with a name? Do six consecutive paragraphs begin with dialogue? Do three begin with a subject-verb sentence construction or a prepositional phrase?

When you alter the construction to solve this problem, do so with care. Don't change them only for the sake of variety. The best way to communicate your story is more important.

Watch for too many paragraphs that begin with a phrase that doesn't include the main subject and verb. For example:

> As George drove to the store, he pondered what Dorothy said.

"He pondered" is the main subject/verb phrase and can stand independently as a sentence. The "as" phrase cannot. It is dependent on the main phrase.

It's fine to begin some paragraphs this way. Just be careful to avoid having more than one or two on a page. If an action is important enough to begin a paragraph, it should usually include the main subject and verb.

Narrative Fragments:

A fragment is a phrase that poses as a sentence but is missing either a subject or a verb.

For example – "Went to the beach."

This phrase has no subject. It doesn't reveal who went to the beach. It is merely a fragment.

I have noticed an increase in the use of narrative fragments in written storytelling. It has become popular as a narrative device because, or so the authors believe, it quickens the pace of the story and provides more of a stream-of-consciousness feel.

I think not.

Fragments are appropriate for use in dialogue and interior monologue because people often speak or think in fragments. They are not, however, appropriate for narrative sections of stories.

My example of "Went to the beach" would be in a narrative section unless it was spoken or thought by a character.

Here is a longer example of narrative text:

> The sun descended below the horizon. Waves lapped against the shore, and seagulls rode the wind with outstretched wings. Ben walked through the sand, his feet bare in spite of the cool breeze. A gull waddled up and bit his toes. Ben kicked it and grinned as the bird fluttered away.

This narrative is easy to understand because every sentence has a subject and a verb.

Here is how a fragment writer might render the same narrative:

> Sun at the horizon. Waves and seagulls. Ben with bare feet. Cold breeze. Kicked a gull. Grinned.

When readers see this, their minds have to reconstruct the thoughts and figure out what's missing. Is the sun rising or setting? What are the waves and seagulls doing? Who kicks the gull? Did Ben grin or did someone else grin, that is, someone who might be watching?

The answers might come to readers in a split second, but that tiny pause slows the reading process. It harms the pace and interrupts the stream of thought. It can confuse and puzzle readers, potentially jerking them out of the story.

Here is an example of a narrative fragment from a work-in-progress someone sent to me.

> The third one paused. Sniffed the air.

"Sniffed the air" is a narrative fragment. It has no subject. Who sniffed the air? Most likely "the third one," whoever it was. But it could have been the point-of-view character who sniffed the air to see if "the third one" was emanating a tell-tale odor. Readers might figure out the correct answer quickly, but the pause to do so slows the story and harms the stream of consciousness.

Why would authors want to take the risk when the perceived benefits of narrative fragments don't really exist and the potential risks are real?

On the other hand, fragments can be put to good use in interior monologue, like this:

> Ben stared at a crab skittering across the sand. A fiddler crab? Maybe. Too dark to tell. Would his toes be in danger? Not to worry. The first-aid kit was in the car only a hundred yards away.

This paragraph begins with a complete narrative sentence that introduces interior monologue. Then the text describes Ben's thoughts in all their fragmented glory. Yet, it is easy to understand because the thought pattern is connected and properly transitioned without need of explanation.

With narrative, the author tells what's going on, and the reader needs subjects and verbs that don't require a pause for interpretation. Since narrative is supposed to paint the scene, precise communication is important.

When an author writes with an intimate point of view, however, sometimes the boundary between narrative and interior monologue can blur. What might be called narrative can actually be what a character is thinking, and in such cases, fragments can be appropriate.

In order to employ interior monologue fragments properly, an author needs to recognize the difference between true narrative and interior monologue that takes on a narrative purpose, that is, describing what is going on.

Here is an example of interior monologue that

tells what's going on, borrowed by permission from a fellow writer's work-in-progress:

> There—through a gap in the trees where another ridge jutted up in the southern distance. Pale bodies coming this way. Heading toward the castle.

Fragments are appropriate here, because these are fragmented thoughts that flow directly from the point-of-view character, and since they describe what is going on, they are narrative in purpose. This is a blurring of the narrative/interior monologue boundary.

Most recent novels I have seen use narrative fragments, making me assume that my opinion is in the minority. Yet, I can assure you that if you follow my advice to shun narrative fragments, your prose will be clearer, and you will avoid the problems that narrative fragments can cause.

Tool #4 - Dialogue Mechanics

Dialogue is a crucial part of great novels, because it injects a feeling of reality. The fact is, most people talk. Some people talk a lot. So in order to make our stories realistic and natural, we need to show people talking.

Yet, dialogue sequences that are badly structured or poorly conceived can be confusing or even make your story unrealistic to the point of absurdity.

In order to make sure your dialogue sparkles, let's first look at how to structure a series of dialogue paragraphs.

1. **Every time the speaker changes, break to a new paragraph.**

I'm sure the vast majority of you already know this, but I receive a surprising number of stories that have multiple people speaking in the same paragraph.

2. **When a particular character's actions and dialogue occur one after the other, if possible, keep the action and dialogue in the same paragraph.**

In dialogue, I like to think of paragraphs as belonging to the speaking character. The paragraph in which a character speaks will also contain that character's actions when the spoken words and action occur in sequence.

For example, from *Reapers*:

> I gave him a casual nod. "What's up, Mex?"
>
> "Glad you recognized me." His usual hint of a southern accent gave away his Texas roots, and his voice jittered as he glanced from side to side. "Listen, Phoenix. I'm in trouble. I need one more soul to meet quota. Just one. Age doesn't matter."
>
> "Okay." I stretched out the word. "Just go to the executions and pick one up."
>
> "It's not that easy." He took a step closer. "I'm on the probation list. Suspicion of trafficking souls."
>
> "Just suspicion, huh?"
>
> "Of course." He glanced both ways again but said nothing more.

Notice that each paragraph includes a character's words and actions. The first paragraph belongs to the "I" character, Phoenix. He nods and then speaks. The second paragraph belongs to the responding character, Mex. He speaks, glances from side to side, and speaks again. The third paragraph reverts to Phoenix again. He speaks, stretches out the word, and speaks again. And so on.

This is another rule that is not hard-and-fast. Sometimes the actions of others might be interspersed within a character's paragraph. This is merely a guideline to help writers remember a structure that is easy for readers to follow.

3. **If you begin a paragraph with dialogue and want to use a speaker tag to indicate who is speaking (like "he said"), insert the tag at the first natural break in speech.**

For example, the following paragraph has the speaker tag near the end:

> "Without a doubt, you are the most gifted candidate to apply in all the years I have been a part of this organization. You have passion, a proven record, and perseverance. If you are accepted, and if you decide to join us, you will certainly go far. Nothing can stop you," Jim said.

In this excerpt, if there are several people in the room, a reader might think a character other than Jim was making this speech. Then "Jim said" corrects the reader far too late, which jerks a reader out of the story. In order to keep the reader in the loop, it is better to put "Jim said" near the beginning, like so:

> "Without a doubt," Jim said, "you are the most gifted candidate to apply in all the years I have been a part of

this organization. You have passion, a proven record, and perseverance. If you are accepted, and if you decide to join us, you will certainly go far. Nothing can stop you."

4. **Sometimes a character speaks for a long time, adds various actions, and continues speaking, all without significant interruption. If you put all of these into one paragraph, the paragraph can become bloated and overly long. Find a way to break up the paragraph.**

For example, here is a bloated paragraph of dialogue:

"I invited you to join us on this dangerous mission," the king said, "because you have proven yourself in battle as well in matters of stealth. We need a man of your talents to gain access to the enemy's gate." He looked over the castle's parapet toward the horizon where the boundary wall lay. "You see, no one has been able to discover the secret entry code, a spoken word that will open the massive door."

Since shorter paragraphs are easier to digest than longer ones, I would break the dialogue into smaller chunks.

"I invited you to join us on this dangerous mission," the king said, "because you have proven yourself in battle as well in matters of stealth."

Sir William bowed his head. "Thank you for the honor, Sire. How may I be of service?"

"We need you to gain access to the enemy's gate." The king looked over the castle's parapet toward the horizon where the boundary wall lay. "You see, no one has been able to discover the secret entry code, a spoken word that will open the massive door."

Watch for dialogue paragraphs that are more than five lines long. These are often better presented in smaller pieces.

5. Said is not dead.

I heard the following story from a writing student: A teacher in a fourth grade class held a funeral for the word *said*. The students put the word in a coffin, threw flower petals on top, and chanted, "Said is dead. Don't use said." In other words, when using speaker tags (often called dialogue tags), like "Mary said" or "Lou said," come up with a more creative verb, like chirped, or guffawed, or giggled.

I hoped that this terrible advice was limited to a misinformed elementary school teacher, but I have since learned that some popular writing-curriculum instructors teach the same thing.

Said is dead?

No. *Said* is very much alive.

Other writing students have told me of teachers who insist on *always* using *said* in tags. *Said* is invisible to readers, so anything else will stick out like a proverbial sore thumb.

Is it any wonder writing students get confused when they hear contradictory advice?

It's true that *said* is usually invisible to readers. But it can also be a flashing siren if it's used too often.

> "Hello," Matt said.
>
> "Hi," Sue said.
>
> "Where are you going?" he said.
>
> "To the store," she said.

See what I mean? Repetition creates the proverbial sore thumb.

But what happens if you follow the said-is-dead rule in the following way?

> "Hello," Matt greeted.
>
> "Hi," Sue chirped.
>
> "Where are you going?" he queried.
>
> "To the store," she rejoined.

Even worse, right?

The authors of *Self-Editing for Fiction Writers* explain this concept well:

> We're all in favor of choosing exactly the right verb for the action, but when you're writing speaker attributions the

right verb is nearly always *said*. The reason those well-intentioned attempts at variety don't work is that verbs other than *said* tend to draw attention away from the dialogue. They jump out at the reader, make the reader aware, if only for a second, of the mechanics of writing. They draw attention to your technique, and a technique that distracts the reader is never a good idea. You want your readers to pay attention to your dialogue, not the means by which you get it to them. *Said*, on the other hand, isn't even read the way other verbs are read. It is, and should be, an almost purely mechanical device—more like a punctuation mark than a verb. It's absolutely transparent, which makes it graceful and elegant. Which, actually, is another reason to avoid explanations and adverbs. Even when you use them with *said* (we said sternly), they tend to entangle your readers in your technique rather than leaving them free to concentrate on your dialogue.[2]

The key to making speaker tags transparent is variation. In dialogue sequences when a tag is needed, *said* is the most invisible and should be your "go-to"

---

[2] Renni Browne & Dave King, *Self-Editing for Fiction Writers*, (New York, HarperCollins, 2014), 89-91

tag, but it is better to employ dialogue beats and skip tags the majority of the time.

> Matt stopped on the sidewalk and smiled. "Hello."
>
> "Hi." Sue adjusted her purse and glanced at her shoes. Why had she worn these old things? *Oh, please don't notice!*
>
> He looked straight at her shoes. "Where are you going?"
>
> "To the store." *He noticed!* Heat rushed to her cheeks. *I'm going to die right here and now.*

This version has no speaker tags. Although it's a silly sequence, you still know who is speaking without the need of tags. The dialogue beats, that is, the phrases that supply action and interior monologue, let the reader know who is speaking. They also add a bonus. Readers can see what is going on and feel the emotion.

Notice that a beat can come before the spoken words or after them. Often a beat can come between two lines spoken by the same person, as follows:

> "I was wondering." He touched his shoe to hers. "Looks like you've got a lot of miles on those. You must be a runner."

The dialogue beat provides a natural pause between two spoken lines as well as a visual cue. Again, no speaker tag is needed. Often, a speaker would naturally pause between two dialogue phrases. That's a perfect opportunity to add a natural action between them.

For example:

"I'm going to add my favorite ingredient. Do you know where the cayenne pepper is?"

Since the speaker would naturally pause between the two sentences, we can insert a dialogue beat to provide the pause as well as a visual.

"I'm going to add my favorite ingredient." He slid out the spice drawer and rummaged through it. "Do you know where the cayenne pepper is?"

I advise using dialogue beats the majority of the time with a sprinkling of speaker tags to vary the structure. When people are not moving, I will use tags like "he said" more often, especially if they are in a dark place and visual movement is impossible to see.

Also, tags are usually unnecessary when only two people are talking, especially when each character has a unique voice.

In addition, using a reasonable substitute for *said* is fine if you do so infrequently. Sometimes my characters will growl or bark their words, but I use such alternatives sparingly so they will be more emphatic when they occur. Also, a few other tags are nearly as invisible as *said*, such as *asked*, *replied*, and *whispered*, so I use them more often than other alternatives.

Some writers, in order to use *said* while giving it more pizzazz, will adorn it with an adverb.

"Yes," she said happily. "I am a runner."

"Cool," he said shyly. "Do you ... um ... want to go for a run with me sometime?"

That's not pizzazz. That's telling without showing, which is inferior writing.

Instead, show happiness in a dialogue beat. Show shyness the same way. Let readers see and feel the emotion instead of slapping on an adverb to tell them the emotion.

> She swallowed, barely able to keep a shout from bursting forth. "Yes. I'm a runner."
>
> "Cool." He folded his hands at his back and averted his eyes. "Do you ... um ... want to go for a run with me sometime?"

One more point: don't use impossible speaker tags:

> "Sure," she grinned. "How about tomorrow morning? I know a great three-mile course."
>
> "Perfect," he smiled. "Seven?"

You can't grin or smile your words. Stay far away from tags like these.

In the above example, you can use the same words properly if you alter the punctuation to change the tags to dialogue beats, as follows:

> "Sure." She grinned. "How about tomorrow morning? I know a great three-mile course."
>
> "Perfect." He smiled. "Seven?"

Here are a few final dialogue tips, some of which I mentioned earlier:

1. **Don't explain the spoken words.**

"Show, don't tell" is crucial in dialogue. Don't tell the emotions.

> "It's the queen scow crow!" Gordon shouted in terror.

"In terror" is a telling phrase. Instead, show the terror.

> Gordon's knees knocked together. "It's the queen scow crow!"

2. **Avoid using adverbs to dress up speaker tags.**

This is yet another rule that is not in the hard-and-fast category. It's just something to watch for.

> "The engine is a goner," Gordon said grimly.

"Grimly" tells that he is grim. Instead show that he is grim.

> Gordon held the charred rotor in his greasy palm and shook his head. "The engine is a goner."

3. **Make the character's spoken words match the character.**

A prim and proper character's speech would differ greatly from a character who tends toward street talk.

"I find it hard to believe that you stooped that low" versus "Dude! What were you thinking?"

4. **Avoid dialogue designed for the purpose of informing the reader.**

This is called "contrived" or "informational" dialogue.

> "Maggie, I know you were my student for three years at Eagle Academy, but you shouldn't be so familiar."
>
> "But I lived next door to you for five years before that. Without you there in the Martian underground, I would have gone crazy."

Since both characters know this information, they wouldn't remind each other of it. This contrivance happens when the author is trying to inform the reader. Since real people don't talk like this, avoid it.

5. **Show interruptions with an em dash. Show intentional pauses or trailing off with an ellipsis.**

> "Maggie! Get the—"
>
> "I have it!" Maggie lifted the slingshot and aimed at the queen crow. "Ready ... aim ... fire!"

Dialogue is a critical means of communication, not just among the characters themselves, but also a way for readers to "hear" what they have to say. While it is true that we want our story's dialogue to be natural, we can't make it as natural as what we might hear in reality.

If you were to go to a crowded restaurant or shopping mall with an audio recording device and leave it on for an hour, then go back and try to transcribe the conversations you heard, you probably wouldn't be able to recognize much of it as rational dialogue.

You would hear interruptions, partial thoughts, quick shifts to off-topic rabbit trails, long-winded explanations that make no sense, and the like. If your story's dialogue looked like that, readers would get frustrated and maybe want to shake a character, shouting, "Get to the point!"

We need dialogue that mimics reality. We achieve this by inserting some of the characteristics of natural conversations. Allow characters to interrupt each other by cutting off the previous speaker's sentence. Let them have an occasional "Um" or "Wait" or "Where was I?" Allow them to be foggy once in a while, prompting another character to ask for clarification.

Yet, don't include too many of these natural missteps or your readers will get annoyed or frustrated. We want to have just enough flaws to make the dialogue sound real but not too real.

Tool #5 - Interior Monologue

I mentioned interior monologue in several places earlier in this book. Although I will repeat some concepts, I think it's important to give this tool its own section and add items that I haven't discussed yet.

Interior Monologue (IM) is expression of the POV character's thoughts, a crucial way for a character to communicate to readers.

Characters think a lot, or at least they should, and readers can't know a character's motivations for many of his actions without a dive into his mind.

Yet, not every thought from your POV character's mind needs to be aired. Only what is relevant to the story should be reported, especially issues that the POV character will react to.

I mentioned that in dialogue, we shouldn't try to show natural conversations, just to mimic their qualities and missteps. The same is true with interior monologue. If we were to express thoughts exactly the way normal people think, we would sometimes write a jumbled mess. Although we can quote exact thoughts from time to time, it's usually better to describe a summary of pertinent thoughts.

In other words, there are two ways to express IM:

1. **A description of thoughts.**
2. **Exact quotes from the mind.**

Here is an example I used in the dialogue mechanics section:

> Matt stopped on the sidewalk and smiled. "Hello."
>
> "Hi." Sue adjusted her purse and glanced at her shoes. Why had she worn these old things? *Oh, please don't notice!*
>
> He looked straight at her shoes. "Where are you going?"
>
> "To the store." *He noticed!* Heat rushed to her cheeks. *I'm going to die right here and now.*

In the second paragraph, readers get a chance to dive into Sue's mind, and she expresses her thoughts in two distinct ways. First we have "Why had she worn these old things?"

This is a thought about her shoes, and it falls into category #1, a description of thoughts instead of #2, an exact quote from the mind.

An exact quote might have been something like, "Oh, no! Why did I wear these old things? They look a thousand years old, like my great grandmother might have bought them when she was a teenager."

Although those words might have flown through Sue's mind in three milliseconds, the details would have bogged down the story, and they weren't important. Instead readers get only the essentials in a summary.

Thought descriptions and exact quotes have three main differences in how we write them.

First, we write descriptions with the same pronouns that we use for our point-of-view choice. If we chose third-person-limited POV, then we use third-person pronouns for the description, e.g. "she" in "Why had she worn these old things?"

Second, we write descriptions with the same tense as we use for our narrative sections. If we chose past tense in narrative, then we use past tense in the thought description.

In contrast, we always write quoted thoughts in first person (when referring to the character being quoted) and present tense. "Why did I wear these old things?"

Third, we write thought descriptions in the same kind of font as we do narrative in dialogue, but we italicize quoted thoughts.

In the example, *Oh, please don't notice,* is the exact wording of a thought, making it a quoted thought. It is present tense and italicized. The next quoted thought is *I'm going to die right here and now*. It is also present tense and uses a first-person pronoun to reference the POV character.

In my earlier books, I often used quoted thoughts,

but I have since reduced them and more often opted for thought descriptions, saving the exact thought quotes for times when I wanted a forceful emphasis.

For example, in Reapers:

> Mex, still holding his clasp, blinked at Bartholomew. "Hey! I'm not feeling any energy flow."
>
> "There is a reason for that." Bartholomew shook the adapter tube. A syringe fell out of the end and dropped to the ground.
>
> I gulped. *My syringe!*

My syringe is a quoted thought directly from Phoenix's mind. If I had chosen a thought description, it might have been:

> I gulped. That was my syringe.

In this case, a quoted thought is a desperate cry and needed more emphasis than a description could have conveyed.

Here is another example from *Reapers* that shows a contrast between the two types of IM.

> I brought the ring to my cheek and rubbed the cool metal against my skin. No matter what Misty did, I would keep our promise. I couldn't let those bitter winds infect my heart. Although Sing and Shanghai were both beautiful young women inside and out, giving in to their charms would break my

only attachment to the days when love still thrived through any storm—days of innocent ignorance, to be sure, but days when I looked forward to each coming dawn. If I broke that connection, all hope that those days might return would be shattered forever.

I shifted the ring to my lips and kissed it. *Yes, Misty, I will keep our promise. I have to keep it. I can't survive without a lifeline to love.*

In the first paragraph, the words after the first sentence were all Phoenix's thoughts, described instead of quoted, past tense instead of present, and shown in a normal font.

In the second paragraph, the words after the first sentence are all Phoenix's thoughts again, but they are quoted instead of described, present tense instead of past, and italicized, and, in this case, they come at the end of a chapter. I hoped that the use of a quote would be an emphatic way to punctuate his sad loneliness in a manner that a description couldn't accomplish.

Take note of the importance of the paragraphs' opening sentences. They introduce the interior monologue, letting us know that the following sentences are from the character's mind. They also provide a hint of the character's mood by showing us actions that reveal a mindset. It's crucial to include these introductions before every interior-monologue sequence.

In summary, interior monologue is essential for describing a character's mindset, moods, and motivations. We need to provide IM every time the POV character's thoughts are important to the story, whether as reactions to what he has seen or heard or as motivations for his upcoming actions.

Tool #6 - Show, Don't Tell

Many aspiring writers hear this phrase often - "Show, don't tell," and rightly so. It is one of the most important lessons we writers learn.

"Show, don't tell" means to provide visual images of what you're trying to describe instead of simply telling a fact in a way that provides no visuals.

For example, a boy might bring his pet frog to school for show-and-tell time. If another student simply told the class about his frog, which presentation would be more vivid and interesting? The one that shows the frog, of course.

Here is a list of some differences between Telling and Showing:

1. Telling describes emotions, attitudes, and objects. Showing brings them to life.

2. Telling is usually a summary description provided by a narrator. Showing is a real-time description that makes the reader feel present in the scene.

3. Telling usually fails to paint vivid pictures in the reader's mind. Showing provides precise pictures.
4. Telling often uses vague adjectives that a reader can misinterpret. Showing evokes adjectives in a reader's thoughts.
5. Telling often fails to incite emotion in readers. Showing provides a character's real-time emotions in a way that provokes similar emotions in readers.

For example, here is a "telling" summary of a job interview:

> Lindsey answered her job interview questions with a confident attitude and informal flair, thinking that familiarity would endear her to Mr. Dawson. Unfortunately, he thought she was overconfident and ignorant.

This summary might be accurate, but does it seem vivid to you? Did it create visual imagery in your mind? Likely not.

Here is another account of the same interview using the "show" method:

> Mr. Dawson folded his hands on the desk and peered at Lindsey through thick glasses. "What experience have you had in video editing?"
>
> "Lots." While Lindsey smacked her chewing gum, she spread out her fingers and gazed at her black nail polish. "I edited bunches of videos for our high school band and track team. Everyone says I'm the best."

"I see." He cleared his throat. "And who is included in 'everyone'?"

"Oh, my friends, the track coach, my mom." She winked. "You know, the important people."

Mr. Dawson smiled with tight lips. "Well, I think a video professional might be more important. Has your work been recognized by anyone in the industry?"

"Sure." She rolled her eyes upward. "I think his name is Ed."

He blinked at her. "Ed?"

"Right. The guy who runs the school's video website."

I'm sure you could "see" this account better than the other one.

"Showing" is usually provided in real-time, that is, as it happens, as if readers are there witnessing the account moment by moment. Telling usually feels like a summary after the fact.

As I mentioned earlier, "telling" often uses adjectives that might not provide specific pictures, while showing gives precise visuals. Here is an example:

> The dog was pitiful, helpless, too crippled to hunt for food.

Pitiful, helpless, and crippled are grammatically correct adjectives, and readers will probably conjure images based on the adjectives, but those images might not match the writer's vision. They won't invade the reader's imagination to paint a precise portrait. Also, "dog" is vague. A visually oriented writer will be more specific.

Here is a "show" version of the same account:

> The golden retriever clawed at his flank, scraping hair from his mangy coat. After licking the wound, he struggled into a hobbling gait. With every stride, he hopped to favor a mangled back leg. In the distance, a squirrel sitting atop a fallen log stared at him. It chittered, then pranced away without looking back.

The second version is far more vivid, because it shows what pitiful looks like. It shows what helpless and unable to hunt for food mean in a visual way.

In other words, instead of telling us that the dog is "pitiful," a writer's goal is to cause the reader to conclude that the dog is pitiful. The same is true with the other adjectives. Draw that adjective from the reader's mind as a conclusion based on images instead of planting the word itself. This method will create sympathetic emotions instead of merely an academic understanding.

Inducing emotions is a crucial storytelling skill. Here is another example.

> I was both furious and downtrodden. I had never felt so awful in all my life.

In this case, the writer tells the emotions to the reader by means of adjectives - furious, downtrodden, and awful.

Okay, we've been told, but so what? Did you feel those emotions along with the character? My guess is not at all.

Let's see what happens when we show these emotions in a real-time scene:

> I slammed the door and screamed, "How dare he call me a tramp!" I snatched my beret off and threw it against the wall. That self-righteous pig! Just because I suggested that we go to his cabin for the weekend, that makes me a tramp!
>
> I stomped into the kitchen and snatched the moose-tracks ice cream from the freezer. I dug the biggest spoon out of the drawer, pried the top off the carton, and gouged out a huge scoop.
>
> As I stared at the chocolate bits in the chunky mass, a tear crept to my eye. The word Why echoed in my mind. Why was my heart thumping so wildly? Why were my ears so fiery hot? Why was I ready to shovel ice cream into my mouth like a spoiled toddler? And most of all, why did I care so much about the cruel label he stamped on my forehead?
>
> I sank into the corner of the kitchen and dropped the spoon into the carton. Because I have no respect for myself? Because I have about as much self-control as a drug addict? I let out

> a long sigh. Because maybe I really am a tramp?
>
> I dropped the carton, curled my legs up to my chest, and sobbed.

Notice that the writer never labeled the emotions (furious, downtrodden, and awful) but instead showed them being acted out. Readers will feel those emotions along with the character as the scene generates sympathy or pity and creates a sense of attachment.

An emotional connection between readers and characters is one of the most important aspects of writing. If you fail to achieve this, your story will feel academic and lack heart-tugging passion.

In short, in most cases, we need to show emotions instead of telling them. Yet, this is often difficult to do, which explains why many authors avoid it, as explained in *Self-Editing for Fiction Writers:*

> It's easier simply to say "Erma was depressed" than to come up with some original bit of action or interior monologue that shows she's depressed. But if you have her take one bite of her favorite cake and push the rest away—or polish off the whole cake—you will have given your readers a far better feel for her depression than you could by simply describing it. People are depressed—or angry or relieved—in their own unique ways, so simply conveying the fact of the emotion to your readers doesn't really tell them who your character is. It's

nearly always best to resist the urge to explain. [3]

It's also important to understand that "showing" is not always the better choice. If you want to quickly summarize a series of events and move on, it's better to tell. You won't create visuals or provoke emotions, but that might not be your goal. If you show every detail, your story might become tedious and tiresome.

In other words, don't show everything, especially when summarizing events that are not critical to your story. Consider telling instead of showing when you have:

1. **Transitions between important scenes.**
2. **Dialogue that retells events that have already been shown.**
3. **Backstory elements that set a scene.**

Transitions between important scenes:

Often you will write a series of important scenes, but the events that occur between the scenes are not crucial. Still, you might want readers to know what occurred. These in-between events are perfect for "telling."

Here is an example:

> At the Zodiac, people embraced, some danced, others just knelt and wept. The fires of liberation were spreading.
>
> During the next hour or so, the liberated

---

3 Browne & King, *Self-Editing*, 16

slaves gathered their few belongings, collected food from the homes of the dead dragons, and distributed it freely to everyone. Arxad, Magnar, Fellina, and Xenith carried the most seriously wounded to the healing waters while the healthy soldiers walked to the river leading to the demolished barrier wall and washed there.

After making sure the wounded had been cared for, Adrian walked toward the barrier river, following a chorus of splashing sounds. When he arrived, he found several soldiers bathing, including Ollie.

"Hey, Adrian!" Ollie tossed a square fragment of soap. "Word has it you're engaged to Marcelle!"

Notice that the first two paragraphs summarized events, while the third transitioned to real time. Then the fourth paragraph settles into real-time showing mode.

Dialogue that retells events that have already been shown:

Sometimes you will have instances in which some characters were away from action you have already described, and the character who was involved in the action needs to inform the others. If that character proceeds to explain, and you provide every word of explanation, readers will find it tedious, because they already know what happened. This is another perfect time for a "telling" summary.

Here is an example:

> Adrian grasped his father's wrist. "It would take a long time to explain what they're all about, so I'd better focus on the most important issues."
>
> "Very well. Let's hear them."
>
> "We have a problem at home. A man named Cal Broder has taken over as governor of Mesolantrum. Arxad thinks he is a male Starlighter who has the power to usurp the king's throne."
>
> After Adrian provided a few more details, his father described how Frederick escaped from his prison of ice as well as how they battled both white and dark dragons all the way from the forest to the village.
>
> When they finished exchanging stories, Adrian exhaled. "Sorry I missed the action."

This sequence begins in real time and introduces the explanation in order to let the reader know which events the character is about to explain. Then the text summarizes the rest of the explanation, thereby avoiding boredom for readers. And again, the final paragraph transitions back to real-time showing.

Backstory elements that set a scene:

Sometimes you will have to inform readers about back story information, especially when you're writing a sequel and the events you wish to convey occurred in an earlier book. A "telling" sequence can serve as a reminder so readers can refresh their memories about crucial facts that will come into play in the scene.

In order to avoid information dumping, make such telling sequences short and infrequent. Readers don't want a full retelling, just a memory prompt.

Here is an example (note that this is from a character's POV who is not mentioned. He is looking on and observing):

> Shellinda and Wallace knelt at the opposite side of the grave, both with tears tracking down their dirty faces and grass staining their trousers. Their rolled-up sleeves revealed grime covering their arms as well, interrupted in spots by a rash—the telltale sign of the fatal disease plaguing nearly all of Starlight. They couldn't stay here to mourn. The only possible cure lay to the north where Cassabrie had flown with Regina's spirit in tow. Dwelling within Exodus, this world's guiding "star," Cassabrie had floated away less than an hour earlier, guiding the buoyant, glowing sphere with her powerful mind. The only sensible step was to follow.

A summary like this should come across as a series of motivations for the actions the characters are about to take. This way, the information feels less like narrator intrusion and more like a character's thinking process. As you might expect, the next paragraph resumes the story's real-time showing mode.

A final word about showing:

Don't show details that aren't important. Some writers think that showing means to describe everything—the color of the carpet, the height of the tree, or the pattern of the ants crawling on the sidewalk. If those details aren't important to the story or a character's inward journey, then it's probably best to leave them out. In other words, as I described in the POV tools section, if the character wouldn't take notice of the details, then don't show them to the readers.

Also, there is no need to show details that everyone will already assume. For example, if you set a scene in a library, you don't have to write that it contains books, shelves, and a librarian's desk. Readers will paint in those details on their own. You should, however, mention details that are unusual or that will come into play as the scene unfolds, such as a shield hanging on the wall that a character will grab to protect himself from flying debris when an explosion erupts.

Show details that are important to the story and/or the character, even the library's books and shelves if they are unusual in some way or create a significant impression. Any details that are mundane and insignificant can be left out.

Readers can also imagine visuals that are commonly recognized. For example, if you read "She gave him a skeptical glance," can you picture the facial changes? Most people don't need written details explaining what a skeptical glance looks like, and describing the bend of an eyebrow and the thinning of the lips might slow the story too much. Also, a reader might misinterpret the "shown" expression. In those cases, you can "tell" when the visual is likely to come into a reader's mind without showing.

The reason we show is not primarily to paint a visual picture, though that is important; it is to set the reader intimately within the scene so that a character's actions, thoughts, and emotions make sense. Since readers want to go on a journey with a character, showing the story through the character's eyes is crucial. Report what is important to the character, which is often considerably less than what is actually within the character's visual senses.

In conclusion, "Show, don't tell" is a great guideline, but maybe a better guideline would be, "Show what is important to the character during critical parts of the story; tell anything else that is necessary for understanding the story."

Tool #7 - Foreshadowing

Foreshadowing is an indication, a sign, or a warning of what is coming in the future. It is an author's way of introducing a later event in a story that might otherwise appear to have popped up out of nowhere.

The concept is fairly simple, but not always easy to employ.

Too much foreshadowing can come across as heavy-handed or overly obvious. Readers might be offended that the author thinks he must reveal so much to his inobservant readers.

Too little foreshadowing can be missed by readers, and the hoped-for effect will be lost. They might think a new device that suddenly crops up is contrived, because they didn't see it coming.

Authors hope to avoid both problems by employing the following foreshadowing rules:

1. **Every weapon, tool, ability, and unusual character should be foreshadowed.**

2. **Show or indicate these devices in an inactive state before they become active.**

3. **Allow their appearance in an inactive state to be incomplete or mysterious.**

As I mentioned in the Ordinary World section, a simple example of rule #1 is a warrior's sword. You should never show a warrior battling with a sword unless you first show the sword in a scabbard at his hip or in some other inactive state.

Imagine reading a story that follows a character for fifty pages, then on page fifty-one, a dragon swoops down and attacks him. He draws his sword and does battle. Yet, the author hasn't mentioned the sword at all before this point. The character just suddenly has it.

That would jerk many readers out of the story. They might ask, "Where did that come from?" It is this question that we hope to avoid through foreshadowing.

Regarding rule #2, showing the sword in battle is the active state. Showing the sword at the warrior's hip is the inactive state. When you write that a warrior is carrying a sword, that reference doesn't raise the "Where did that come from?" question. Readers accept device introductions in an inactive state. Once the device has been introduced, it can be activated, and readers know where it came from.

The inactive state has many options. The sword might not be at his hip. It could be hanging on the wall or embedded in a dead soldier's chest. The key is to show it on the wall or in the chest before the warrior needs it for battle.

Rule #3 is optional, but it can be powerful. Suppose that the warrior battles by playing music rather than slashing with a sword. Instead of a sword, he carries a flute. Since the flute's battle purpose isn't obvious, you can be mysterious and not reveal its use completely until the time it becomes active.

Yet, you still need to show the flute in its inactive state, and you should provide hints regarding its power. If people ask the warrior about the flute, he can be coy or quote an old prophecy that merely hints at its use. He might play a tune that makes people uncomfortable, which implies that the flute has some sort of power beyond producing music.

Then when a battle comes, you can show its full power. Since you have established that it has supernatural abilities, readers will expect more.

Any story element that feels like a surprise should be foreshadowed. For example, in my book *Starlighter*, Koren comes upon a building and notices its features:

> She pressed her forehead against two cool bars and peered in between. A semicircular apse lay at the far end of the high-roofed building, the Separators' meeting place where, according to the theories of some slaves, they determined Promotions and many Assignments. Behind that, a lofty dome with a central belfry towered over the rest of the building. The bell inside rang at midday and also whenever a Promotions ceremony had ended. Now it was time

to find a way in to see all these mysteries for herself.

This foreshadows the fact that the building has a bell in a tower.

In another passage, she notices something else that becomes important later:

> A light flickered from somewhere within the Zodiac's deep recessed portico. Someone was at work, studying the stars, their positions, their movements. Was it Arxad? Had he been unable to sleep? It wouldn't be unusual. He often wandered the corridors of his cave and sometimes journeyed back to the Zodiac if something troubled his mind.

This foreshadows that Arxad, a dragon, might be nearby.

Together, these two passages create a foreshadowing setup that includes a bell and a character in inactive states.

Later, both devices become active and the foreshadowed elements appear:

> She looked back across the Separators' assembly room. A dragon-like shadow in full flight appeared in the opposite corridor. Was it Maximus?
>
> With a quick jerk, she lifted the lantern's glass and blew out the flame. She leaped into a sprint, the fire behind

her providing enough light. Soon, the walls curved, blocking the assembly room's firelight.

Once again probing the dark air with her hands, she slowed. Her fingers struck something solid, a flat wall. A dead end! Yet, something fibrous brushed her face. It moved easily from side to side. Was it a rope?

She set the lantern down and grasped the rope, a braided cord too thick to wrap her fingers around, but a series of knots helped her get a grip. With her first pull, the rope descended with her weight. A loud gong sounded above. Then, the rope jerked her upward, and another gong reverberated all around.

Koren grimaced. A bell! She scrambled up the knotted cord. If she could just—

A gust of wind blew her hair. As a third gong sounded, something sharp clawed the back of her shirt and yanked her away from the rope and into the air. She flew into the upper chamber and fell to the floor on her backside. A dragon landed next to her and shouted, "Fool of a girl!"

Koren pushed with her feet and slid away, but when the dragon's face clarified, she stopped. "Arxad?"

If I had failed to show the inactive bell in advance, Koren's accidental use of the bell would feel contrived. If I had not suggested that Arxad might be near, his sudden appearance would have come out of nowhere.

Yet, the passage about the inactive bell did not reveal how it would activate. The reference to Arxad did not tell readers that he would rescue Koren. Still, the bell and Arxad were placed in readers' minds through foreshadowing, so they became allowable tools for future activation.

Besides avoiding reader frustration, foreshadowing also adds connection and cohesiveness. Good foreshadowing makes the story feel like more than a jumble of events. The pieces feel joined in an orderly manner.

The connection also adds to a sense of fulfillment, that ideas come to fruition, that apparent randomness has a goal or purpose. Readers might not sense this cohesion consciously, but they will notice its absence if story elements fly in at random or if foreshadowed elements never come to pass. In such cases, readers have an innate sense that something is wrong. Most are uncomfortable with a chaotic world.

Many authors enjoy adding twists to their stories, that is, events that surprise readers, often at the climactic stage. We want readers to gasp and say, "No! That didn't really happen!" This creates a spike in emotions that helps make your story memorable.

Since we want to surprise readers, we might wonder if we should foreshadow story twists. Will foreshadowing ruin the surprise and minimize or eliminate the desired gasp?

We should definitely foreshadow twists. Otherwise, we will annoy readers. While they might enjoy being surprised, they don't want to be betrayed. They don't want to be shocked by something they couldn't possibly see coming, that is, a shock that is unreasonable, out of the blue, or a violation of the elements you have set in the story.

For example, if your hero dies, that is often a big twist that readers might not accept. If a piano randomly falls from a window and smashes him, and no story-related reason exists for the death, then readers might throw your book across the room. Yet, if he dies because of a carefully prepared series of events that aids the story, then readers can accept the tragedy even if they are shocked by it.

Still, you can foreshadow a twist without giving it away. This will protect your desire to deliver a gasp while avoiding reader annoyance.

In *Reapers*, I foreshadowed the death of a certain character. As you read, you can tell that this character might die, so there is no surprise when he or she actually dies. The twist is how the death comes about. In other words, I foreshadowed the death, but readers likely did not expect the method. Yet, if readers mentally recall the events leading up to the death, they will likely nod and think, "Yes, it all makes sense. I should have seen that coming."

And this is the key. We don't want readers to see the twist coming, but we do want them to believe that they *should* have seen it. Every twist should adhere to the story's foundational elements, and the twist must have a purpose. If the twist ignores either of these maxims, readers will feel betrayed.

In the film *Tangled*, a story twist raised a literal gasp in me. When Flynn Rider (Eugene) cut Rapunzel's hair, his action shocked me. What a great twist! Why was it great? Because, although I didn't see it coming, it took only seconds for me to realize how well it worked in the story. The writer foreshadowed every element of the twist without giving the actual twist away.

Although Rapunzel's hair was a treasure of priceless value, it was also the reason for her captivity. The only way to set her free was to separate her hair from her. Also, Flynn's story arc demanded a redemptive act, one that could not be denied. He believed that rescuing her would result in his death, but love and a redeemed heart combined to launch his compassionate and selfless act.

The story foreshadowed the cutting's effect on her hair and on the villain. It foreshadowed the crippling of her healing ability. It even foreshadowed the tool Flynn would use to cut her hair, a fragment from the broken mirror, which was also an appropriate symbol.

The setup was perfect. The action was flawlessly executed. The twist was gasp-inducing. Yet, I never saw it coming. And afterward, I muttered the appropriate line: "I should have seen it coming."

Without the foreshadowing, the twist would have been flat and ineffective. Foreshadowing made it powerful and memorable.

The next sequence in the film, however, bothered me greatly. After such brilliant storytelling, I felt betrayed by how the script writer saved Flynn's life through healing by Rapunzel's tears. After viewing the film a few times, I still couldn't see how it was foreshadowed.

One day I decided to sit down and watch the film, searching for any foreshadowing of this scene. I couldn't believe that a talented writer would omit such an essential element.

It didn't take long to see it. A drop falls from the sky. When it hits the ground, it creates a healing flower, which foreshadows the teardrop falling from Rapunzel's eyes and healing Flynn. After the teardrop falls, at the site of his wound, you will see a burst of light that takes the shape of the healing flower.

The foreshadowing is there, and it is beautifully done. I just missed it. My feelings of betrayal were wiped away. This story is exceptional because the writer employed foreshadowing with deft expertise through every sequence, including the stunning twist and healing.

Your writing method will affect how you insert foreshadowing. Since I don't outline my stories before I begin writing, I have no idea what will happen until it happens, which means I don't foreshadow anything while writing the first draft. I have to go back and write the foreshadowing in later, and that takes a lot of time.

Writers who outline have an advantage in that they can insert foreshadowing as they write, knowing that the warrior will draw a sword or play a weaponized flute in whichever chapter they planned the action. Their disadvantage is that their first drafts will require a lot more planning in advance, which means that outliners do the extra work up front, and seat-of-the-pants writers like me do the extra work on the back end.

Either way, foreshadowing is a must, and if we want readers to stay hooked, we can't risk jerking them out of our stories with lack of foreshadowing.

That wraps up the toolbox section of this book. I hope the tools have helped you write readers into your story. Keeping readers "inside the skin" of your characters will supercharge their enjoyment, and they will come back to enjoy your works again and again.